Joyful En   n
hug from   g
her own l.. journey and those of several saints, Maria Gallagher reveals how Mary is perpetually teaching us, loving us, and leading us to her Son, through every up and down, twist and turn of life, always enveloping us in her gentle embrace. Mary's role in our own lives is beautifully illuminated and the reader is led to a deeper and more profound experience of praying the Rosary.

— **Bonnie Finnerty**, member of the Harrisburg Diocese Catholic Women's Conference Committee and host of the podcast "Positively Pro-Life."

Like Mary is the bridge to Jesus, Maria Gallagher's book becomes the bridge to Our Queen. In sharing her own personal struggles with raw honesty and grace, she draws parallels to the saints and the Joyful Mysteries, inspiring us to embrace them in new and profound ways. A truly blessed read!

— **Claire McGarry**, author of *Grace in Tension: Discover Peace with Martha and Mary.*

Joyful Encounters with Mary will help you cultivate a powerful, deep relationship with Mary, who in turn will lead you to God. Maria Gallagher shares reflections on the Joyful Mysteries of the Rosary, a road map for cultivating virtue, holy saints to emulate, and heartfelt stories from her own life as she invites women to journey with Mary through the highs and lows of life.

> — **Patrice Fagnant-MacArthur**, author of
> *Our Lady of La Salette: A Mother Weeps for Her Children.*

This is the spiritual companion you didn't know you needed. Maria Gallagher gives women the opportunity to slow down and examine the life of the Blessed Mother through each Joyful Mystery, using personal stories, the lives of the saints, and gentle questions to guide the reader into a deeper relationship with Mary and, ultimately, her Son. *Joyful Encounters with Mary* moves beyond our rote recitation of prayers to living the scriptural mysteries alongside Mary, guiding women to reflect on how they can model their own lives after hers.

> — **Carolyn Astfalk**, Catholic novelist, writer, and blogger (CarolynAstfalk.com).

Joyful Encounters with Mary

A Woman's Guide to Living the Mysteries of the Rosary

Maria V. Gallagher

Available from:
Marian Helpers Center
Stockbridge, MA 01263

Prayerline: 1-800-804-3823
Orderline: 1-800-462-7426
Websites: ShopMercy.org

Library of Congress Catalog Number: 2022933899
ISBN 978-1-59614-560-3

Publication date: April 30, 2022

Imprimi Potest:
Very Rev. Kazimierz Chwalek, MIC
Provincial Superior
The Blessed Virgin Mary, Mother of Mercy Province
February 2, 2022
Feast of the Presentation of the Lord

Nihil Obstat:
Robert A. Stackpole, STD
Censor Deputatus
February 2, 2022

MARIAN PRESS
STOCKBRIDGE MA 01263

TABLE OF CONTENTS

INTRODUCTION
Joyful Encounters with Mary

I will never forget the first moment when I longed for an encounter with Mary. I was six years old, standing on tiptoe to reach the bathroom sink. My mother was beside me, gently and conscientiously brushing my teeth — a technique I had not yet mastered, despite having already learned useful skills such as reading and arithmetic.

I began to sob inconsolably, much to the confusion of my mother, who was, after all, just trying to aim a toothbrush at my molars.

"What's wrong?" she asked, an expression of concern and compassion flooding her Irish eyes.

In between heaving sobs, I managed to cry out, "I want to see Mary!"

She knew instantly that I was not talking about my Aunt Mary, nor the Mary who had befriended me in my first-grade class. I was referring to *THE* Mary, the Mother of Jesus, my patron saint.

Here I was, after a long day of school and miscellaneous shenanigans, demanding a vision of Our Lady. I had often seen my mother grasping her Rosary beads, silently praying for the intercession of her Queen. I figured my Mommy had an "in" with the Blessed Mother and that she could somehow make Mary appear before my very eyes.

My weary mother hustled me to bed, and I knew that I would not see Mary that night. But I held out hope that someday, somehow, I would become the next St. Bernadette and have a Lourdes-like vision to call my own.

It was my father who had introduced me to the whole idea of apparitions. One of his favorite films was a classic black-and-white drama called "The Song of Bernadette."[1] Starring the luminous actress Jennifer Jones in the title role, the movie told the story of St. Bernadette's encounters with the Blessed Mother in Lourdes, France. I was enchanted by the other-worldly image of Mary appearing in the grotto before Bernadette's amazed eyes. I wished in that moment that I could be Bernadette, conversing with Our Lady. To this day, the film moves me to tears of joy.

I realize that it often takes a certain combination of humility and holiness to be a visionary like St. Bernadette — a status that I am unlikely to achieve in this lifetime. And yet, I have experienced my own joyful encounters with the Blessed Mother, both in contemplating the mysteries of the Most Holy Rosary and in seeing the threads of those mysteries in the course of my life.

From pregnancy to childbirth, and from accompanying my daughter during rites of passage to locating her after she went missing, I have experienced a taste of the Joyful Mysteries of the Rosary. In reflecting on various incidents in my life, I can see how, though I will never achieve her sinlessness, I share similarities with the Blessed Mother. Having consecrated myself to her Immaculate Heart, I can also see her influence on my life, with both its triumphs and tragedies.

And I firmly believe that, if you look closely enough, you, too, can see Mary's hand amid your daily struggles and achievements. True, you may never view Mary's indescribably beautiful image before you, but you can still experience a powerful relationship with her, if you are willing to take the time and make the commitment.

Mary can be your heavenly confidant, your best friend, and your go-to saint for those times when you need someone to intercede for you before the throne of God. This can be true, even if you did not grow up with a deep devotion to Mary, are a convert struggling with Mary's role in salvation history, or experienced a strained relationship with your own mother (or have little, if any, relationship at all).

In short, this is a book for all female seekers of Mary, from the simply curious to the strongly committed. We can all learn from Mary, whose ultimate goal is to point us to her Son, Jesus. In forging or strengthening our relationship with Christ's mother, we will enhance our relationship with God, the whole reason for our being.

Some people consider Mary to be an obstacle to Jesus — as if she somehow blocks our path, making it difficult for us to see Him. They believe that devotion to Mary lessens their connection with Jesus. They feel as if they must choose between Mary and Jesus as they live out their spiritual lives. In other words, they believe that you can either belong to "Team Mary" or "Team Jesus," and never the twain shall meet.

But I have learned from the teachings of the Catholic Church — and my own experiences with Mary — that Mary does not block the way to Jesus. In fact, Mary is a bridge to the second Person of the Most Holy Trinity. She enters our lives not to interfere with our relationship with Jesus but to enhance it. Indeed, I've never felt closer to Jesus than I have since dedicating my life to Mary. She is the star that illuminates the path to the Lord, helping us along the way to salvation. She takes nothing away from Jesus but rather helps us to build a solid foundation for a close relationship with Him. Mary is the gateway to Christ at every stage of our lives.

In the words of St. Louis-Marie de Montfort, "To Jesus through Mary!"[2]

Your encounters with Mary can be every bit as inspiring as a Hollywood production — even more so, because they will be utterly unique and completely personal. The more you find yourself meditating on the Joyful Mysteries of the Rosary, the more you will see how the mysteries relate to your own life. Along the way, you just may find yourself growing in virtue and conquering many of the vices that have stood in the way of your personal relationship with Jesus.

Mary is not our Savior — that is a title reserved for Jesus alone. But she is the self-described "hand-maid of the Lord,"[3] and she can help us to become better servants of God. She leads not only by the example of her life but through her intercession for us before our Heavenly Father. With Mary by our side, we can conquer the sin in our lives, grow in the supernatural virtues of faith, hope, and charity, and achieve a more open, honest relationship with Jesus.

This book explores the Joyful Mysteries of the Rosary, but that is not to say that Mary skipped merrily through the events that are depicted in these decades. In fact, each mystery carries with it challenge and even pain, uncertainty, and loss. And yet, Mary's joy could not be stolen from her, despite the hardships she faced. It is this buoyancy of spirit that we can learn to imitate as we carry the crosses that fall along life's path.

So, come journey with me as we explore Mary's life and, in so doing, gain greater insight into the mysteries that fill our days. We are fellow seekers as we travel the way of holiness and redemption.

Personal Reflections

1. Have you ever thought of your life as a mystery? What are the mysteries you are facing at this time in your life?

2. What word would you use to describe your current relationship with Mary? How would you like to relate to Mary — as a mother, a friend, a trusted guide?

3. What experiences brought you joy this week? Can you detect Jesus' presence in those experiences?

4. Reflect for a few minutes on the last 24 hours. In what instances did you act as a servant of the Lord? How could you have been a better conduit for God's mercy and love?

CHAPTER 1
The Greatest Expectations

I would estimate that, at any given time, at least a half-dozen dolls decorated my bed when I was a little girl. The collection made me feel maternal and quite protective of my make-believe family. In Sunday school, I was enamored by a lesson in which the protagonist adopted ten children of various races and ethnicities. A huge family, I thought, was my destiny.

The dream of achieving family bliss by supersizing intensified after I grew up and was engaged to be married. One of my best friends, who was also a bridesmaid, predicted that I would give birth to 12 wild boys. Whether by birth or by adoption, a family of at least "Brady Bunch" proportions was definitely on my homemaking radar.

I had made the decision that I would relinquish my journalism career so that I could stay home and take care of what I imagined to be a bustling brood. Financial pressures, however, made it impossible to quit my job after I married. The financial squeeze, in fact, was so intense that I pursued Natural Family Planning (NFP) in an effort to delay pregnancy.

I found our NFP classes fascinating. I had been woefully ignorant of how the female body functioned, as far as reproduction was concerned. Our patient NFP instructors, a lovely couple with a picture-perfect family, explained how to spot the signs of fertility. Although I was a novice at fertility awareness, I quickly got into the habit of charting my daily temperature and examining cervical mucus to determine when I was most likely to conceive. Avoiding marital relations during times of fertility was a challenge but one I readily embraced, thinking that I was doing what was best for my future family.

And yet, the longing for a child was palpable. I would see the neighbor's children playing in the yard, and a wave of sadness would wash over me. Years passed, and the longing simply strengthened. To me, it was not a question of *if* I would have children – but *when*. The maternal urge was strong within me.

I worked as a radio reporter, and I recall one Valentine's Day when I reported to a school to gather interviews for a feature on the holiday. As I walked into the elementary school classroom, I noticed the children were fascinated with my microphone and tape recorder. The students swarmed around me like honeybees, eager for their treat.

I asked them a series of questions about love and Valentine's Day, and I was impressed by the answers. I also experienced a profound sense of gratitude for having the opportunity to be with children. I didn't want the feeling to go away. I wished that that beautiful moment, surrounded by those sweet children, would last forever.

Finally, after three years of using NFP to delay pregnancy, my husband completed his doctoral program and was hired for a position out-of-state. We made the decision to end the waiting game and to use what we had learned as a result of NFP to attempt to conceive a child.

After such a long period of childlessness, I was eager to end my child-free days and to embrace full-time motherhood. I assumed that the first month that I engaged in the marital embrace during signs of fertility, I would become pregnant.

But my body did not conceive a child on demand. I remember the pain and confusion I experienced when, at the end of the month, my menstrual period returned. The cycle repeated a second month, then a third. I was beginning to wonder if I could conceive at all.

I will never forget an especially painful night when I experienced yet another round of bleeding. I cried out to God, wondering why He could be so cruel as to prevent me from realizing my dream of being a mother. The emotional turmoil was indescribable. Rather than patiently accepting my plight, I struggled against the cross I had been handed.

And then, quite mysteriously, the bleeding abruptly stopped. I wondered what was going on with my body. I was both confused and curious, but also, a bit hopeful, thinking that my dream of a pregnancy finally might be realized.

I had been volunteering at a local pro-life pregnancy resource center, assisting women facing unexpected pregnancies. On a whim, I asked a seasoned pregnancy center volunteer if I, myself, could take a pregnancy test. She readily agreed and, much to my surprise and unending delight, I discovered that I was indeed pregnant.

It was in that moment that my anger at the Almighty melted. I had achieved my life-long dream, and a new, precious life was tucked safely away in my womb.

I consecrated my pre-born baby to the Immaculate Heart of Mary, invoking Mary's protection for my son or daughter (although I wanted twins, I sensed somehow that that was not a possibility with this pregnancy). I had consecrated myself to Mary some years before, using the formula outlined by St. Louis-Marie de Montfort, and I so wanted my child to feel Mary's loving embrace, as well.

As an expectant mother, I drew even closer to Christ and became an even more devoted follower of Mary. I gave up the soda that seemed to continually course through my system and instead opted for good old water. I followed a high-protein diet that had been recommended by my childbirth educator.

I remember being so hungry that I raced through a Mexican restaurant drive-thru, gobbled my tacos, then drove through the line a second time to try to satiate my pre-born child.

I was a mother on a mission, determined to do what was best for baby.

I also had a heightened sense of the dangers to my pre-born child that seemed to lurk everywhere. Was I eating something that could harm the baby I desperately wanted to meet? Were there toxins in the household cleaners I was using that would pose trouble? My worry list seemed to grow longer by the day.

And yet, I also felt a sense of peace, that Jesus and His mother were watching over me. That feeling became more pronounced the day my car skidded on the wet pavement, and I ended up doing a complete 360-degree turn — without hitting another car. It was miraculous to my mind and a sign that God was in protective control.

Perhaps you have known the unbelievable thrill of being pregnant, of holding an unrepeatable cherished life within you. Like Mary, you became an instrument of Christ's love in the way that you cared for your pre-born baby. Mixed with that joy, you might have also experienced the fear of the unknown, which was also apparent to Mary at the Annunciation.

If you have suffered the loss of a baby to miscarriage, I invite you to reach out to Mary and allow her to minister to you in your grief. She is the ultimate mother, and she stands ready to care for you with tenderness and conviction.

If you have experienced an abortion, know that Mary can be your greatest ally, helping you to deal with the intense emotional pain. Hope and healing are available to you, no matter where you are on your path of grief. (To learn about the Rachel's Vineyard program of healing retreats, visit rachelsvineyard.org)

But what if you have never experienced a pregnancy? It is still possible to see the threads of the First Joyful Mystery of the Rosary in your life. Think of a time in your life when you prepared for a big event — a tournament, a graduation, a wedding. Did you feel the excitement build as you readied your mind, body, and spirit for that incredible milestone? At times, did you wonder whether your "big day" would ever arrive? Did you invoke God's help and protection as you made your preparations?

As women, whether or not we actually give birth, we are all called to be spiritual mothers. It is our task to "aid mankind in not falling,"[4] as the Second Vatican Council proclaimed. When we think of all the troubles that face our world today — civil and political unrest, racial tensions, the "culture of death" identified by Pope St. John Paul II — planet Earth could definitely use our motherly touch. We are called to tap into the feminine genius Pope St.

John Paul II wrote about so eloquently and use it to ennoble our families, our workplaces, our schools, and our communities.

We can achieve great spiritual growth as we are waiting in a garden of expectations. As we bring our prayer requests to God through the hands of Mary, we learn persistence in prayer. We have faith that our prayers will be answered according to God's perfect timing. We trust that He is listening and taking note of our appeals, and that He will respond at the time and in the manner that is best for our souls.

I have to admit — the waiting can be quite challenging. I have harbored in my soul one special prayer request for 13 years. I realize that God has richly blessed my life, but I still hold out hope that he will someday grant my particular request. I have not abandoned hope; therefore, I have not abandoned prayer. I am hoping that the current answer to my prayer is "wait" rather than a firm "no."

Perhaps you are in a similar position. Maybe you have a desire deep in your heart that you long to be fulfilled, but you need God's help to realize your dream. Know that I am praying for you — either for the wish to be granted or for you to accept the plan God has for you. The waiting game can be easier to play, knowing that we have people who will cheer us on. One of those people is the Blessed Virgin Mary, who cares for you with a deep and abiding love. In the next chapter, we will reflect on Mary's wait for her Son and Savior to be born.

Personal Reflections

1. If you have experienced pregnancy, what was the experience like in a spiritual sense? Could you find yourself growing closer to God?

2. If you have never experienced pregnancy, what situations in your life have required you to wait extensively for an event to occur?

3. Looking back, can you see how God accompanied you in the waiting room? In what ways have your waits been like Mary waiting for Jesus to be born? In doing this reflection, do you find yourself drawing closer to Mary?

4. Do you have a special prayer intention that has gripped your heart for a long time? What do you think God might be communicating to you now, as you await your answer?

CHAPTER 2
Encountering Mary at the Annunciation

The angel Gabriel was sent from God to a town of Galilee called Nazareth, to a virgin betrothed to a man named Joseph, of the house of David, and the virgin's name was Mary[5].

As a first-grader, these words captivated me. I was fascinated with angels, and was known to pretend to be one on occasion. There is something so inherently pure and elegant about the concept of an angel.

In the *Catechism of the Catholic Church*, we learn, "the existence of the spiritual, non-corporeal beings that Sacred Scripture usually calls 'angels' is a truth of faith. The witness of Scripture is as clear as the unanimity of Tradition."[6]

As we reflect on the First Joyful Mystery of the Rosary, we can picture Mary as a young teenager, shocked to find an angel before her. It is an awe-inspiring moment — an unforgettable glimpse into the world of the supernatural. The angel is a messenger of God, a harbinger of things to come. We can imagine Mary being overwhelmed, wondering why she would be honored by an angel's appearance. This would be one of the many moments that she would ponder in her heart.

To a large extent, Mary seemed to have her life planned out. She was engaged to Joseph the carpenter — we can envision her dreaming of what married life with her beloved would have been like. She must have had certain expectations about what lay ahead.

And then an archangel named Gabriel arrived and rocked her world.

As the archangel came to her, he said:

"Hail, favored one! The Lord is with you."[7]

A complimentary greeting to be sure, one that paid tribute to Mary's vast well of grace, otherwise known as the life of God within her. If she had any doubt that God was beside her and, indeed, within her, that uncertainty must have melted away in Gabriel's presence, right?

Well, not immediately, as Scripture tells us:

But she was greatly troubled at what was said and pondered what sort of greeting this might be.[8]

Was Gabriel friend or foe? Was he a heavenly creature or a follower of Satan? What was his aim in visiting her? Perhaps Mary had an intuition that her life was about to be shaken, upended, and rearranged. Her expectation of a simple life of domestic bliss with her Joseph would have to be set aside because of what her mysterious visitor was about to say.

> "Do not be afraid, Mary, for you have found favor with God."[9]

At this point, we can imagine Mary saying to herself, "O.K., go on … "

> "Behold, you will conceive in your womb and bear a son, and you shall name him Jesus. He will be great and will be called Son of the Most High, and the Lord God will give him the throne of David his father, and he will rule over the house of Jacob forever, and of his kingdom there will be no end."[10]

This Scriptural passage possesses a great deal of material to unpack, so let's look at it line by line, verse by verse.

As is often the case in Scripture, a call is issued to not be afraid. We can imagine that, in Mary's case, this was far easier said than done. After all, out of nowhere, an archangel had come before her. I think the typical human response to such an event would be jaw-dropping fear.

But Gabriel is a creature who always acts in perfect surrender to God's gracious will, and he is urging Mary to do the same. He tries to allay her fears by noting that God is pleased with her. But then comes the earth-shattering, soul-gripping news that she will conceive and bear a son named Jesus.

Though Mary was young, she was not naïve. She knew that, in the order of things, virgins did not conceive and bear children. Medically speaking, it was impossible.

If Gabriel had stopped there, it would have been enough of a shock to Mary. But he continued on, indicating that she was to be the mother of the offspring of the Almighty. She might have thought to herself that such a chain of events was impossible, that she, the humble Mary, was in no position to bear and raise the Savior of the world.

Mary then forthrightly expresses her skepticism, saying,

> "How can this be, since I have no relations with a man?"[11]

Mary confirms her virginity, but it is not an impediment to God the Father's wondrous plans, as the Archangel Gabriel explains.

> "The Holy Spirit will come upon you, and the power of the Most High will overshadow you. Therefore the child to be born will be called holy, the Son of God."[12]

As we would say today, that was the "mic-drop moment." Gabriel made it clear: Mary was to be the mother of God's Son. The holiest man to ever live was to be born of a lowly virgin. It's a wonder Mary did not pass out from fright right then and there.

And yet, the surprises kept on coming, as Gabriel explained,

> "And behold, Elizabeth, your relative, has also conceived a son in her old age, and this is the sixth month for her who was called barren; for nothing will be impossible for God."[13]

The miracles would not end with Mary. Her cousin Elizabeth had already received a long-awaited miracle — a son she could call her own, despite her advanced age. It is one thing to say that nothing is impossible for God; it is quite another to witness the statement in action. Soon, Mary would see for herself that Elizabeth was with child, fulfilling the promise of the angel.

Still, for the Incarnation of Jesus to occur — for God to descend to earth and become man — Mary's consent was critical. This consent, known as her *fiat*, has inspired generation after generation to say "yes" to God — even in the most difficult of circumstances.

The words Mary said next helped to open up the gates of Heaven to you, me, and all those who would have otherwise been locked out of paradise because of the original sin inherited from Adam and Eve.

"Behold, I am the handmaid of the Lord. May it be done to me according to your word."[14]

Mary views herself as a servant, prepared to perform whatever act the Lord commanded. She seeks nothing for herself — she has no interest in fame and fortune. She realizes how rich she is in the blessings that Almighty God has bestowed upon her. She is ready to be God's vessel, to pour out for Him the love that fills her soul. She knows the power of God's word, and she longs to fulfill it. He need only speak, and she will act.

Wouldn't you want such a person as your friend?

Personal Reflections

1. Has this chapter caused you to look at Mary in a new way? How so?

2. Are you experiencing fear right now in your life? Do you struggle with the concept of trusting God?

3. Can you see Mary as a "bridge" to Jesus? What concern would you like to entrust to Mary's care?

4. Can you see yourself as a servant of the Lord? What would it take for you to achieve such a role in your life?

CHAPTER 3
Growing in Virtue: Humility

T radition has it that the fruit of the First Joyful Mystery of the Rosary is humility.

Ah, humility.

I had a chance to listen to an audio recording of my parents and me, taped when I was four years old. I could hear my mother cheerily say, "Here she comes!" as I bounded up to the tape recorder.

I then launched into a rendition of one of my favorite pop songs at the time, belting out each note with *gusto*. You could just hear the pride in my voice as I pretended to be a pop music princess.

But I was no Britney Spears. In fact, listening to my vocals was as painful as having a spear slice through my ear. I could not get over how wrong I had been about my singing ability. Granted, I was only four, but still — couldn't I have had more self-awareness? Or more talent?

Yes, pride has reared its ugly head many times in my life. I was a classic perfectionist in school, weeping profusely if I scored less than 100 percent on a test. My demand for perfection led to a multitude of tantrums and other flights of drama, with my poor parents and sister suffering from the fallout of each episode.

My desire to excel might have been laudable, but I took it to the extreme, resulting in a fair share of misery in my home. I look back on those days and cringe because I can see now how much I put my poor family through.

The irony was that my parents were not demanding when it came to grades — their philosophy was "do the best you can." They had both been academically minded when they were in elementary school, but they exerted zero pressure on my sister and me to perform well in school. My drive to be perfect stemmed from something deep inside me: a fear that catastrophe would occur if I could not ace every exam, every assignment.

I falsely surmised that, if I failed to achieve academic perfection, I would never graduate from college ... never have a decent job ... never succeed in life. It was as if I believed that all my dreams would be shattered if I scored an 85 percent on a single quiz.

It would be years before I would realize that the root of my problem was pride — a word I had always associated with school spirit and family loyalty. Somehow, during my 11 years of Catholic education, I had failed to grasp the concept of the capital sin of pride.

As the *Catechism of the Catholic Church* states, capital sins "engender other sins, other vices."[15] I especially appreciate the *Catholic Answers* definition of pride: "the excessive love of one's own excellence."[16]

Perhaps one of my most memorable manifestations of pride came during my senior year in high school. I dreamed of attending a certain college with a legendary history of achievement. But, to do so, I thought I had to win a similarly legendary scholarship, which would pay for the entire four years of tuition, room, and board.

One day at school, I learned I had not been awarded the coveted scholarship. Ironically, my mother was picking me up from class early to take me to a luncheon for a women's club that was presenting me with an award for scholastic achievement. The minute I got into the car, I started bawling, unable to contain my emotions. I had zero gratitude for the award I was about to receive. I had already lost the big prize — the full scholarship to a high-status university. My mother could not console me because I refused to be open to hearing her healing words. I wanted to drown in a sea of self-pity, and I had no interest in coming up for air.

In that moment of defeat, my petty pride was on full display. I found it difficult to accept the idea that my plan was not the same as God's plan. In the exam called "Life," I felt I had received an "F" in bright red ink.

In later years, I would view the loss of that scholarship as a gift from God. I ended up attending a university close to home, where I could pursue my passion for journalism. I blossomed as an anchor for the school radio station and then went on to work as a professional broadcaster. Such a wonderful experience might have never been realized if I had followed a different academic path.

Social media can exacerbate the problem of pride. We may think we need to "keep up with the Joneses" social media posts. We see a Pinterest-perfect holiday meal online and think we have to not only emulate it but better it. This can lead to another vice — envy. I recall once seeing an Instagram post about a reality TV star's second vacation home. I was filled with envy, thinking how nice it would be to not only have a vacation home, but a *second* vacation home to call one's own. How could I possibly compete, knowing my social media posts could not compare with hers?

The antidote for pride is the virtue of humility. As you can imagine, I have had difficulty with the concept over the years. To me, humility meant groveling, timidity, and life as a doormat — an unappealing proposition.

However, as I learned more about the Catholic faith as an adult, I realized that my concept of humility had been all wrong. My spiritual director, a priest who has since passed away but whose words of wisdom linger with me still, explained that humility was the truth, no more, no less. It meant acknowledging my weaknesses but not negating my strengths.

When we discuss pride, we are not talking about a healthy self-image or a surge of confidence. I once heard humility defined as not thinking less of yourself but thinking of yourself less. In other words, humility does not forget your strengths, attributes, and achievements. It recognizes the truth, but it doesn't exaggerate. Humility allows us to see that there is a God — and we are not He!

I found his perspective to be quite freeing and incredibly helpful to my spiritual growth. It meant that I was not to think less of myself, but rather that I should stop obsessing about myself, particularly about my imperfections. St. Thérèse of Lisieux, often described as "The Little Flower," came to see her faults not as sources of shame but as cause for rejoicing. Imperfections mean that we must rely on the Perfect One, the Almighty, and the grace He provides for our salvation.

In meditating on the lives of Jesus and Mary by praying the mysteries of the Rosary, we can grow in our appreciation of humility. The First Joyful Mystery shows us Mary in a vulnerable state, shocked by the visit of an archangel. She does not react pridefully, saying, "How dare you mess up my plans!" Rather, she gratefully accepts God's plan for her life, trusting Him with the results. She is an instrument in His hands, much like Mother Teresa's comparison of herself as a pencil to be used by God as He wills.[17]

How can we leave pride behind and grow in humility?

- Pray for the grace to increase your humility. But be prepared — you can expect God to permit situations that cause you to swallow a few pieces of humble pie. This can be a highly challenging experience, but God will give you the grace to see it through.

- Keep in mind the words that God said to St. Catherine of Siena: "You are she who is not, I am He Who is."[18] Recognize, as Mary did, your role as a creature, brought to earth by the Divine Will. We can do nothing without His help. Every breath we take is a result of His assistance.

- Recite the Litany of Humility (included at the end of this book) once a week. You may be surprised how much it helps you to keep things in perspective. It is a tremendous prayer for fostering a spirit of surrender.

- Bear wrongs patiently. You might consider offering your emotional pain for a special intention, such as for the Holy Souls in Purgatory. It can be so tempting to complain loudly when we are unfairly criticized. But remaining civil can be a powerful example of Christian living for others in our lives.

As you pray the First Joyful Mystery, meditate on Mary's humility. Consider how she humbly accepted the shocking words of the Archangel Gabriel. Think about the fact that she did not grumble about God upending her plans but quickly acquiesced. Recognize how she calmly accepted the fact that God was in charge and that He knows best.

Personal Reflections

1. Do you struggle with the vice of pride? Think of ways that you can overcome your prideful moments and demonstrate true grace.

2. Let someone go ahead of you in the supermarket checkout line — and smile while doing it.

3. What portion of the Litany of Humility resonates with you? Why do you find it so compelling?

4. Ask God to show you ways in which you can show humility this week.

CHAPTER 4
Saintly Encounter:
Saint Bernadette

S he was a poor peasant girl, the eldest in a family of nine children. Born in 1844, she did not seem the type of person destined for worldwide fame.[19] And yet, her name has become synonymous with the miraculous, and she has been heralded by clergy and lay people around the globe.

Saint Bernadette Soubirous experienced her joyful encounters with Mary when she was a young teenager, going about her chores in the town of Lourdes, France. She was not looking to make history or to cement her spot as a saint. She was just going through her normal routine when God intervened through an apparition of the Blessed Mother.

As documented by *Catholic Online*, Bernadette caught a glimpse of the beautiful woman as she appeared before a grotto known as Massabielle. Our Lady carried with her a stunning, gold and ivory colored Rosary and was arrayed in clothing of blue and white. And on that February 11th in 1858, a beautiful friendship blossomed between Mary and Bernadette.[20]

A week later, Mary had persuaded Bernadette to return to the grotto each day for a fortnight. With the visions came instructions for Bernadette to drink the spring water that miraculously flowed there — a testament to the divine power that flowed through the grotto.

What captivated Bernadette was Mary's other-worldly beauty, along with her beatific smile, which captured Bernadette's heart. In an appearance that would change the course of Bernadette's life — and the course of world history — Mary informed Bernadette, "I am the Immaculate Conception."[21]

The significance of this phrase was unknown to Bernadette, but it would be a powerful sign to the clergy who later questioned her about the apparitions. Four years earlier, Pope Blessed Pius IX had proclaimed the dogma of the Immaculate Conception, which means that Mary was conceived without the stain of original sin. The fact that Bernadette was unfamiliar with the term added more evidence to the reliability of the apparitions, since she could not have come up with the phrase on her own.

Remarking on the Blessed Mother's beauty, Bernadette said it was "so lovely that, when you have seen her once, you would willingly die to see her again!"[22] The joy that Bernadette experienced in her exchanges with Mary is profound. As is always the case with the Blessed Virgin Mary, her appearances pointed Bernadette to her Son, Jesus.

In her private writings, Bernadette stated, "O Jesus, I would rather die a thousand deaths than be unfaithful to you."[23]

The joy Bernadette found led her to dedicate her life to the Blessed Mother and Christ, the Anointed One.

"O my Mother, to you I sacrifice all other attachments so that my heart may belong entirely to you and to my Jesus."[24]

While Bernadette is known for her simplicity, she had the wisdom to recognize the fact that the joy she experienced with Mary was a foretaste of heavenly splendor.

"I shall do everything for Heaven, my true home. There I shall find my Mother in all the splendor of her glory. I shall delight with her in the joy of Jesus himself in perfect safety,"[25] Bernadette said.

Bernadette's interactions with Mary sustained and strengthened her devotion to God, as evidenced by these words:

> From this moment on, anything concerning me is no longer of any interest to me.
> I must belong entirely to God, and God alone. Never to myself.[26]

It would be wrong to assume that Bernadette experienced a life of ease after seeing the apparitions of the Blessed Virgin Mary. Her own family tried without success to stop her from going to the grotto. She had been diagnosed with severe asthma, and health problems plagued her for her entire life. Some citizens of Lourdes falsely assumed she suffered from mental illness and tried to have her committed to a psychiatric facility. She faced hostility from those who believed the falsehood that the apparitions were a sign of her own grave sinfulness. Diagnosed with tuberculosis, she died at age 35 following a severely painful illness.

From poverty to disease to false accusations, the crosses St. Bernadette had to bear were heavy indeed. Yet, she retained a joy of spirit stemming from her encounters with the Blessed Mother.

In a sense, Bernadette experienced the First Mystery of the Holy Rosary during her visions of the Virgin. Mary's appearance in her life heralded the beginning of Bernadette's humble service of sharing Christ with the world. By sharing her visions, Bernadette became an effective evangelizer — something to which we are all called to be as baptized Christians.

In the midst of sorrows, Bernadette found joy in the love of Jesus and Mary. Her legacy can be seen over the centuries in the throngs of people who have come to Lourdes to seek healing in its life-giving waters. While seekers may or may not find the miraculous physical cures for which they are searching, they may come away with a spiritual healing beyond their dreams.

Personal Reflections

1. Are you familiar with the book *The Song of Bernadette* by Franz Werfel (1941) or the 1943 movie of the same title? If so, what appeals to you about St. Bernadette? If not, what have you learned here about Bernadette that you can apply to your own life?

2. What does Mary's title of "Immaculate Conception" mean to you?

3. Have you ever been so captivated by beauty that you experienced sheer joy? Explain what that experience was like.

4. What would it mean for you to find joy in the midst of your suffering?

CHAPTER 5
Girlfriend's Guide to Connections

The memory is etched in my mind like a carving on an old, solid oak tree. I was in my bedroom, on my cellphone, eager to tell my friend Selena of my pregnancy.

The response was not what I had expected.

"I'm pregnant, too!" she said, and I could picture her smile as I heard her cheery voice.

We were hundreds of miles apart, but we were closely connected — by our pregnancies, by our hopes for the future, and by our faith. She was the first to offer me a remedy for my morning sickness (really all-day sickness): graham crackers (that ended up being my go-to morning snack during the course of my pregnancy).

In Selena, I found a pregnancy buddy who offered me support and unconditional love during the most memorable time of my life. Joys multiplied, and crosses seemed to be cut in half, with Selena only a phone call away. As an older mother, I felt like Elizabeth, with Selena ministering to me as Mary had cared for her cousin.

We ended up giving birth just three days apart, with Selena going into labor ahead of me. God blessed her with a lovely girl she named Jane, while God granted me the privilege and honor of becoming mother to a sweet gal I named Gabriella.

Selena and I were girlfriends, but more importantly, we were soul sisters, striving to be the best Catholic mothers we could be. We commiserated over breastfeeding struggles, diaper deluges, and mountains of laundry. We were joyful comrades in both motherhood and the Church and shared stories of our babies' developmental milestones.

I call these "Mary Moments": grace-filled opportunities to share the Gospel in a concrete way. Over the years, as our babies have grown, our hearts have also swelled with the love of Jesus and Mary that we share.

"Mary Moments" are precious because they help to strengthen our connections not only with other women on earth, but with Mother Mary in heaven. They fill us with joy because we know we are helping other women achieve their potential. The ability to serve is a phenomenal gift, and research in the area of positive psychology indicates it can even help alleviate a case of "the blues." In giving of ourselves to others, we solidify our own sense of self-worth. We can imagine the Blessed Mother smiling above us as we pursue Mary Moments here below.

Reaching out to a woman during her pregnancy can be a powerful Mary Moment. If you have ever assisted a sister, daughter, cousin, or friend who was carrying a child, you realize the power of that experience. It is a true work of mercy to watch a mother's other children while she is going to her obstetrical appointments ... to bring her care packages of protein bars and homemade soup during her third trimester ... to wipe her brow during the stages of labor.

If you are in search of such a mission of mercy, you might consider volunteering at your local pregnancy resource center. These centers of companionship accompany women on their pregnancy journeys, giving them support at a critical time in their lives and the lives of their pre-born babies. Volunteer opportunities run the gamut, from sorting baby clothes and fielding calls to meeting with clients to assess their needs. Many Mary Moments occur between volunteers and clients, helping to form what can become life-long bonds.

We also need to recognize that Mary Moments can occur in the aftermath of a woman's grief following the loss of an unborn child to miscarriage. All too often, women feel isolated and alone following such a tragedy. It is important that we are willing to run to the side of these women, as we can imagine Mary would do. We can help to comfort them in their sorrow ... take care of household tasks that may be causing them stress … and lend a loving, helping hand wherever and whenever needed. We can help a mother rediscover her joy and the beauty of life when she has undergone the suffering of miscarrying a child.

Special attention also needs to be paid to women who have undergone abortions. Research shows that between 30 to more than 60 percent of women who experience abortions were pressured into the decision by someone in their lives — a boyfriend, husband, parent, grandparent, or someone else.[27] Even if they freely chose to abort, they may be mired in an ocean of sadness and regret for their role in the death of their own child.

As Pope St. John Paul II wrote, "If you have not already done so, give yourselves over with humility and trust to repentance. The Father of mercies is ready to give you his forgiveness and his peace in the Sacrament of Reconciliation."[28]

We can minister to women who have had abortions by stressing to them that they are beloved by the Almighty, Who is eager to forgive. No sin — not even the sin of abortion — is beyond His mercy.

I recall a woman named Jennifer whom I met outside an abortion facility. She came to the sidewalk outside the front entrance and dropped to her knees in prayer, tears cascading down her face. I went up to her to try to comfort her, and she told me that she had a friend who had been hurt by the abortion center.

As I began to speak to her, her tear-soaked eyes grew wide, and she said to me apologetically, "I'm sorry I lied to you. I was the one who had an abortion." She then described the process to me in vivid detail; it was apparent that it had been a highly traumatic experience for her. Thankfully, I was able to connect her with a counselor specializing in abortion trauma who was able to guide her through the grief process.

Jennifer happened to attend my parish church, and I saw her one day in the church parking lot, smiling with a friend. At that moment, I was thankful to God for extending to her the healing she so desperately needed.

Jennifer was the first woman I had ever met who had had an abortion. She would not be the last. Over the years, I have met many such women. I admire how they have been able to recover from their grief and now minister to other women with a profound sense of love and humility.

We can sometimes struggle over whether we have just the "right" words to say to a woman facing emotional pain. At such moments, we need to "let go and let God," knowing that He can give us the words we need. It is also true that, at times, words are not necessary. A simple smile can convey the love that an individual needs at that particular moment.

I am reminded of the national Cursillo movement, a movement within the Church to bring more souls to Christ through prayer, study, and evangelization.[29] During the Cursillo Encounters I have attended, people from all different parts of the country and various backgrounds have come together to share the Catholic faith. While some are native English speakers, others speak Spanish, Portuguese, Chinese, and other languages. It is remarkable how well we can communicate with each other with a smile or a laugh. At such times, we realize that there is more that connects us than divides us.

Mary Moments can also occur when women serve as spiritual mothers in reaching out to other women. I discovered this phenomenon first-hand during the Coronavirus pandemic. To combat social isolation and fear, a group of women in my parish began praying the Rosary together in cyberspace via Facebook chat. They found the experience to be so empowering that they added a Divine Mercy Chaplet at 3 p.m. and a nightly novena at the end of the day.

The electronic communal prayer became so popular that they outgrew Facebook chat and graduated to a video conferencing platform to accommodate more attendees. The connection was powerful, as woman ministered to woman with the love of Christ.

The group prayed with each other through the struggles of their lives — from health challenges and loved ones' addictions to pandemic-related stress and relationship struggles. They prayed a special St. Monica Novena for family members who were no longer active in the faith, praying as St. Monica had done for her beloved son, whom we know as St. Augustine.

At no time was the group stronger than when they recited a prayer to St. Gerard, patron saint of pregnant women. One of the group members had mentioned that her daughter-in-law was in danger of losing her unborn baby. The group lifted the young woman up in prayer on a daily basis and, thanks be to God, she delivered a beautiful baby girl.

But the prayers did not end there. The baby was born at a mere 27 weeks gestation and weighed just a little more than two pounds. The group vowed to continue to pray for her until she could return home from the neonatal intensive care unit. Each developmental milestone the baby was able to achieve brought joy to the group and encouraged them to continue on the path of prayer.

With each Hail Mary the group said, they have grown closer to the Blessed Mother and to her Son. They have also formed an unbreakable bond with one another, leading to faith-sharing outside of prayer time. They celebrate birthdays together, plan movie outings, and find various ways to enjoy nature together. Both within and outside their prayer circle, they are evangelizing and finding joy in the process.

Personal Reflections

1. Have you ever reached out to a pregnant woman in need? What was the experience like?

2. Have you had the privilege of encountering a "Mary Moment" recently? How has it strengthened your faith?

3. Who are the "Elizabeths" in your life who could use your concrete help?

4. Would you consider reaching out to other women in your life to join in prayer for some special intentions?

CHAPTER 6
Encountering Mary at the Visitation

G rowing up, I thought the Blessed Mother was something of a superhero, with incredible powers of stamina and strength. After all, while pregnant, she was able to travel the distance to her cousin Elizabeth's home and then care for Elizabeth for an extended period of time. But it seemed as if my mother possessed the same superhero powers because she seemed tireless in her ability to take care of family and friends.

Whether it meant giving her foster mother a manicure or taking her brother-in-law driving in preparation for his road test, she was always willing to lend a hand, with a memorable smile to accompany the good deed. She even expanded her family in a sense by taking on the role of "room mother" at my school. Whenever there was a class celebration, my mother was at the ready with decorated cupcakes in hand. Perhaps superwoman tendencies are common among women of great faith who are dedicated to serving the Lord.

Of course, there was something special about Mary: sinlessness. While we cannot hope to achieve such status, we can, in fact, emulate the Blessed Virgin Mary in her encounter with Elizabeth.

Let's take a closer look at what Scripture tells us about that amazing meeting.

> During those days Mary set out and trav-
> eled to the hill country in haste to a town
> of Judah ...[30]

Certainly, it was not easy for Mary to launch her journey to Elizabeth's home. It was an act of incredible faith and overwhelming love. How many of us, when pregnant, would have wanted to begin such a journey? And yet, Mary did not hesitate. In fact, the text makes clear that she traveled "in haste." She was a woman in a hurry, all for love of God and neighbor. When called to do the Lord's work, we must be ready to act at a moment's notice in service to the Lord.

When she reached her destination, Mary "entered the house of Zechariah and greeted Elizabeth."[31] We can envision the warmth of that meeting of the cousins who shared both history and heritage. We can imagine the excitement of Mary, seeing her pregnant kinswoman. And it can be concluded that Elizabeth was greatly comforted by Mary's visit.

Next, we see the impact the very sight of Mary has upon Elizabeth. "When Elizabeth heard Mary's greeting, the infant leaped in her womb ..."[32]

We have to keep in mind that two people were greeting Mary — Elizabeth and her unborn son. It is significant that the first individual to recognize Mary's beloved Son was a pre-born baby. Saint John the Baptist literally leapt for joy at the arrival of the Savior and His mother.

> And Elizabeth, filled with the Holy Spirit, cried out in a loud voice and said, "Most blessed are you among women, and blessed is the fruit of your womb."[33]

God was definitely with Elizabeth that day — in more ways than one. Jesus was before her, tucked safely in the womb of His mother, and the Holy Spirit was with her, as well. The experience was so joyful it caused Elizabeth to cry out "in a loud voice." Her words would be remembered by future generations as she recognized Mary's unique place in history and among the female population.

Elizabeth is astounded by the turn of events, remarking, "And how does this happen to me, that the mother of my Lord should come to me?"[34]

Mary's cousin demonstrates her own humility and graciousness in this question, noting her personal unworthiness before the Lord. Elizabeth seems awe-struck by Mary's pregnancy and pays her the honor that is due the Mother of God. She further calls Mary "blessed" for having believed in the promises of the Lord.

Mary responds with a beautiful tribute to God that we know as the *Magnificat*, or "Canticle of Mary."

This brings to my mind a memorable visit I made to the Sacrament of Reconciliation. As I confessed my sins, I felt free, for the first time, to reveal to the priest the physical and emotional abuse I had undergone at the hands of a loved one. I now realize that I was not responsible for the physical and emotional abuse I had endured, and looking back I realize that the priest understood my pain. As I related the story, I could see a tear fall from the kind priest's left eye. He told me that the abuse had to stop. It did when I left the abusive situation.

The priest advised me to read and meditate on the *Magnificat*. I drew tremendous power and strength from the reading, and it gave me the grace I needed to cope in the days ahead.

If you have experienced any form of abuse, I encourage you to seek the assistance of a wise professional counselor who can help you navigate through your emotions. Be sure to surround yourself with a support network to which you can turn in the aftermath of the mistreatment. Finally, consider spending some time pondering Mary's *Magnificat* for the spiritual solace it provides.

The *Magnificat* begins, "My soul proclaims the greatness of the Lord; my spirit rejoices in God my savior. For he has looked upon his handmaid's lowliness; behold, from now on will all ages call me blessed."[35]

Mary is, in fact, the new Eve — the woman who will untie the knot created by Eve's disobedience in the Garden of Eden with her own *fiat*. She is filled with joy at the thought of the grandeur of God and knows that, in Him, she will find lasting happiness and peace. While humbly recognizing her place before God, she also recognizes the tremendous blessing God has bestowed upon her by making her the mother of His beloved Son.

> "The Mighty One has done great things for me, and holy is his name. His mercy is from age to age to those who fear him."[36]

Mary gives God the Father the honor that is due Him for the many wondrous deeds He has performed for her. He is Holiness itself, and He bestows His mercies upon all generations.

> "He has shown might with his arm, dispersed the arrogant of mind and heart. He has thrown down the rulers from their thrones but lifted up the lowly."[37]

Mary respects the strength of the Almighty and knows that the arrogant are no match for Him. Kings have succumbed to His power — in fact, any power they hold is the result of His permissive will. God has raised up the humble, affirming them and empowering them.

> "The hungry he has filled with good things; the rich he has sent away empty. He has helped Israel his servant, remembering his mercy, according to his promise to our fathers, to Abraham and to his descendants forever."[38]

Mary notes that God remembers the poorest among us and showers His blessings upon them. He has been a faithful God to Israel, honoring the pledges He made to Abraham in the Old Testament. These are not short-term promises but will be honored into eternity.

We learn from Scripture that Mary stayed with Elizabeth for three months. We can imagine Mary humbly taking on the household tasks of cooking and cleaning. She served without complaint and with abundant grace. In ministering to her relative, Mary exhibited great perseverance, strength, and hope.

Personal Reflections

1. Did you ever undertake a long journey on your own, as Mary did? What did you learn about yourself through the experience?

2. Have you selflessly given of your time to a relative or friend in need? If not, what is holding you back?

3. Are you or someone you know a survivor of a form of abuse (physical, emotional, spiritual)? How have you or your friend been able to cope? Do you see God's hand in your recovery or the recovery of your friend?

4. Was there a time in your life where you felt among the lowly? How did God lift you up?

CHAPTER 7
Growing in Virtue: Charity

I was a young teenager when I learned my younger sister and I had a "ballerina benefactor."

We were in our apartment when the doorbell rang unexpectedly. My mother answered the door, and the delivery man presented her with a large package, addressed to my sister and me from an attorney's office. We couldn't wait to find out what was inside.

We opened the package and found a multitude of savings bonds that had been purchased by my mother's cousin Valeria before she had died. It seemed like an endless stack. When we counted it up, we realized we now had thousands of dollars' worth of savings bonds in our possession.

We had had no idea that Valeria was purchasing savings bonds for us. In fact, we had never personally met her; she lived across the country, in Arizona. My sister and I knew just three things about Valeria: she regularly called my mother to chat, she had been a ballerina when she was young, and she loved my mother dearly.

My parents later took my sister and me to the bank, where we used the savings bonds to purchase a certificate of deposit — our first large financial trans-action. I was overwhelmed by Valeria's generosity and pledged to pray for the happy repose of her soul.

At that point, I fully intended to use the money for my college education in a few years.

But my sense of generosity was tested when my father came to me later with an urgent plea. He and my mother were facing dire financial struggles, and he asked me, as the eldest child, if I would be willing to give my parents the money that Valeria had bequeathed to my sister and me.

I have to admit, I did not want to. I thought back to the day that the package had arrived in the mail and my excitement at seeing all those savings bonds. I thought to myself, "This gift is mine, and I don't want to give it up!"

But I looked at my father and realized with what humility he came to me and that he would have never asked for the money if the need was not great. I granted his request, and our family was able to survive the tough financial times. A bond formed between my father and me that could never be broken, for we had withstood financial calamity and come out safely on the other side.

I wish I could say I was a cheerful giver, but I was not. It's a struggle with which I continue to this day: the ability to be generous, just like my bal-lerina benefactor. I recall a few years ago going to

Confession, and the priest wisely diagnosed my chief spiritual malady: lack of charity.

As an antidote, he gave me an unusual penance: I was to sit in church for a half-hour and thank God for my blessings. I wondered how I would be able to fare. A half-hour seemed like an interminable period of time to discuss with God my reasons for gratitude.

But I surprised myself and was able to list a multitude of blessings, from good health to safe travels to the lovely trees that dotted my path. It seemed as if God had bestowed upon me an endless list of blessings — in fact, a half-hour did not cover it all.

And, as a result of my penance, I felt more inclined to share my riches with other people.

Valeria demonstrated true love of neighbor — a love that spanned the distance of nearly 2,000 miles, from Phoenix, Arizona to Columbus, Ohio. She loved my sister and me, without even seeing us. Certainly, I can return the love of my Heavenly Father, Whom I cannot see, by bestowing love on my neighbor before me.

There are many ways in which we can increase the sense of charity in our souls.

For instance, we can simply pray to God for an increase in charity. God hears every prayer and wants good things for us. He desires that we grow in love and become the mirror image of His beloved Son. If we discover more opportunities to be charitable, we will stretch our "charity muscles" and become stronger in our love of neighbor.

We can also volunteer our time. Giving of ourselves is a powerful safeguard against selfishness — the enemy of charity. I found that volunteering at a pregnancy resource center helped to open my mind and my heart to the plight of women facing challenging pregnancies. In ministering to women in their time of need, I was also able to help their pre-born babies. Volunteering at a soup kitchen, food bank, or homeless shelter can expand our love, too, as we begin to see Christ in the eyes of the poor.

I have also found that I can foster a sense of charity in my soul by resisting the urge to speak negatively of other people. Gossip is a real plague today, especially with all the opportunities for "trash talking" on social media.

As Pope Francis said in a 2020 address, "When we see a mistake, a defect, a slip of a brother or sister, usually the first thing we do is go and tell others about it, to gossip. And gossip closes the heart of the community, disrupts the unity of the Church."[39]

Notice that the Holy Father says that gossip "closes the heart." It is indeed an obstacle to charity and puts us in a position where we judge others based on limited information. There is a great deal of difference between gossip and speaking the truth in love to someone close to us who may be on a dangerous path. For instance, it would be an act of charity to inform our sister or brother that a conversation had been hurtful to us. In all circumstances, love should be our motivation for how we deal with others.

The internet can be a source of great temptation to spew bitter words at Facebook "friends" or Instagram or Twitter "followers." A good rule of thumb may be to ask ourselves the following questions before we post a comment: Is it necessary? Is it kind? Is this the best forum to express this particular viewpoint?

Many people decry the lack of civility today in politics. Politics is the art of the possible, and it can only thrive with the consent and the affirmation of the governed. But I have come to realize that promoting civility begins with me. I need to take full ownership of my words and hold myself accountable. I need to look at those with political differences as brothers and sisters in Christ, rather than as enemies. I need to be generous with my praise and sparse with my criticisms. In this way, I can demonstrate a generosity of spirit that can prove to be contagious, bettering my corner of the universe.

Joyful encounters with the Blessed Mother can definitely deepen our charitable tendencies. We look to her for inspiration and as a model of tireless self-giving. When we consider the sacrifice that Mary made in order to assist her cousin Elizabeth, we are more likely to give of ourselves to other people.

Rather than diminishing our emotional reserves, self-giving can lead us to joy. Think of a time when you helped another person, whether it was in your family, among your friends, or in your community. Did you experience an upsurge in happiness, knowing that you had brightened another person's day? What if we made self-giving a daily part of our lives? Wouldn't our level of joy rise exponentially?

It should be noted that there is a distinct difference between giving of ourselves and depleting ourselves. We must cling to the virtue of prudence and maintain balance in our lives. Rather than strive to become the volunteer of the century, we should not shortchange our own health and well-being as we strive to assist others.

I am reminded of when my baby was first born and I was nursing her around the clock. A wise pediatrician noted that I needed to make sure that I was eating enough nutritious food to sustain both the baby and myself. I was focused so much on breast-feeding that I was not paying enough attention to my own nutritional needs.

New mothers need to be especially cognizant of this type of situation. Remember that Scripture tells us to "love your neighbor as yourself."[40] That does not mean we should neglect ourselves and our physical, emotional, and spiritual needs. In taking good care of ourselves, we can better serve other people.

A quote from St. Teresa of Calcutta, who was known during her life as Mother Teresa, perhaps says it best: "And it is not how much we give that counts, but how much love we put into the giving."[41]

Personal Reflections

1. Have you had benefactors during the course of your life? What did they teach you about charity?

2. Have you ever volunteered for a cause about which you cared? What was the experience like?

3. What concrete steps can you take to avoid gossip in your life?

4. How can you strike a balance between caring for yourself and caring for others?

CHAPTER 8
Saintly Encounter:
Saint Jacinta

I had never heard of the apparitions at Fátima until I was an adult. If they were mentioned in my religion classes, I must have been staring out the window at the time, for I do not recall hearing about Mary's miraculous appearances in Portugal until well after my college graduation. My initial reaction was: Why don't more people talk about these spectacular visions of the early 20th century? Are other people as ignorant of these amazing occurrences as I am?

So, I was completely surprised when I first read about the life of Jacinta Marto, who was born on March 11, 1910.[42] Jacinta admired her cousin Lucia — so much so that she was willing to tag along with the ten-year-old on a sheep-herding expedition. Jacinta's older brother Francisco was also in attendance. The trio relished their time in nature, and Jacinta went so far as to give names to each of the sheep, treating them as friends. The trio liked to pray an abbreviated version of the Rosary, reciting the words "Our Father" once per decade and then the words "Hail Mary" ten times for each bead of the prayer chain. They figured the accelerated prayers left them more time to play.

One spring day in 1916, an angel made an appearance before them in a grove of olives, inviting them to pray.[43] In the middle of summer, the angel reappeared, only this time the encounter took place in Lucia's garden, at a well. There, the angel encouraged the children to offer their hardships up to God in order to spiritually benefit the souls of sinners. At summer's end came a jarring appearance in which the angel was holding a sacred host that was bleeding over a chalice.

In May 1917, in the midst of World War I, the Blessed Virgin Mary made her first appearance to Jacinta, Lucia, and Francisco. She warned the children that they would have to suffer much but tempered that prediction with this telling line: " … the grace of God will be your comfort."[44]

Jacinta was a talkative child — so talkative, in fact, that she told her family about the apparitions, even though Lucia had warned her against telling anyone about what they had seen. She deeply regretted having revealed the secret and was tight-lipped after that. Many of the townspeople and clergy doubted her account, and Lucia's mother became visibly angry about the visitations.

And yet, Jacinta and the other children were not dissuaded from their belief that they had experienced a heavenly phenomenon. In the third apparition, the children were exposed to a vision of hell. The vision inspired little Jacinta to undertake various penances — everything from skipping lunch to wearing a knotted rope around her midsection. She experienced these mortifications for the benefit of poor sinners, in the hope that they would avoid an eternity in hell.[45]

On the day of the final apparition, October 13, with tens of thousands of people in attendance, the Blessed Mother appeared to the young people as Our Lady of Mount Carmel and Our Lady of Sorrows. In addition, the children saw St. Joseph with the child Jesus in his arms, offering a blessing.

That auspicious day, the "Miracle of the Sun" occurred. It was actually raining when, suddenly, the sun peaked through and began to spin through the sky. Witnesses began running for their lives as the sun appeared to be hurling through the atmosphere but then, just as suddenly, returned to its usual spot. The sun dried the soaked clothing in a seeming instant — in what would be further evidence of a miracle.

After this event, Jacinta was much sought-after for her prayers of intercession. One report indicates she may have actually bilocated to assist a young man who was lost in the woods in finding the path home to safety.

In her initial visitation, Our Lady had said she would take Jacinta and her brother home to Heaven in short order. Francisco died in April 1919, while Jacinta perished in February 1920; both deaths were the result of influenza. Lucia, in contrast, lived a long life as a Carmelite nun, returning to the Lord in 2005 at 97 years of age.[46]

Pope St. John Paul II beatified Jacinta and Francisco in May 2000, while Pope Francis canonized them 17 years later, on the 100th anniversary of the first Fátima apparition. The canonization took place in Fátima at the Basilica of Our Lady of the Rosary, a fitting place to recognize the saintly nature of the two seers. In 2017, Lucia was named a Servant of God, the first step in her canonization process.

While Jacinta had much suffering to bear in her brief life, we can surmise that she found a special joy in her meetings with the Blessed Mother. Her love for Our Lady was profound, and it intensified her devotion to the Rosary. In St. Jacinta, we have an inspiring model of piety and fortitude: a young girl who lights our path to Mary and, in turn, to her Son Jesus.

Personal Reflections

1. Were you familiar with the story of Fátima before reading this account? What strikes you most about the apparitions?

2. While few of us will ever have the chance to see the Blessed Mother in this life, many can find evidence of her influence. When did you feel the presence of Mary in your life?

3. Jacinta overcame her talkative nature to become a better servant of God. Is there some fault with which you are now struggling? Would you consider praying for the intercession of St. Jacinta for your need?

4. Jacinta embraced hardship for the sake of the kingdom of God. What penance could you undergo this week for the benefit of poor sinners?

CHAPTER 9
Motherhood Moments

I will never forget the time my mother related to me her experience of giving birth. Her baby — me — arrived early — so early that she did not have time to make it to the hospital. As a result, my father delivered me, with the obstetrician giving him directions via phone.

Home births were not that common in those days, and my mother felt that some people looked down on her for having birthed a baby in her apartment. Still, my mother's light blue eyes lit up as she talked about holding her baby in her arms for the first time.

Although my mother was very articulate, words seemed to fail her as she tried to describe the experience. She then said that, when a woman gives birth, she "just feels as if she has been given a great gift." The value of that gift, to my mother, was priceless.

My mother's second pregnancy was highly challenging. Her obstetrician scheduled a C-section in an effort to preserve my mother's health and the baby's, as well. My little sister Terri was born prematurely and had to be placed in an incubator. My mother and father were quite distressed, not knowing if their baby girl would survive. Thankfully, my sister thrived under my mother's loving care, far exceeding the doctor's expectations.

My mother tended toward pessimism, having been raised in volatile circumstances. Her mother and father both became ill when she was eight years old, and she was sent to live with an aunt in another city. After a brief period of time, her aunt, who was advanced in age, concluded that caring for a little girl was too much for her. My mother then went to live with a friend of her mother's, a woman I came to know as my Grandma Hazel.

A widow trying to raise her own pre-teen girl, Hazel was a stern taskmaster in those days. While I am convinced that she loved my mother greatly, she practiced a "tough love," which made my mother highly skeptical of the world around her. My mother seemed to struggle with showing affection, and she tended to be quite anxious and fearful about the future.

But I believe that, in her two children, my mother found great joy. One incident in particular from my childhood stands out in my mind. A fierce rainstorm was pelting our car, which my mother maneuvered into a parking spot across the street from our apartment building. My mother got out of the car and opened up the rear door so my sister and I could climb out.

The standing water was up to my mother's ankles, and I expressed my dismay at stepping onto the rain-soaked pavement. There was no imminent danger — only a lot of water — and my mother found the situation comical. She began to laugh, which, in turn, made me laugh. In that pouring rain, my mother found a moment of joy — and that moment has stayed with me to this day.

My mother also looked to the Blessed Virgin Mary as a role model, confidant, and protector and discovered joy in that relationship, as well. At age 79, as she lay dying, she prayed for the intercession of the Blessed Mother with the help of a hospice chaplain. And in those prayers, my mother found peace.

I inherited my mother's anxiety, which made motherhood a daunting proposition. My labor and delivery lasted 36 hours, and I opted against taking anything for the pain. But when my baby girl was finally nestled beside me to nurse, I felt a tremendous wave of joy and gratitude for the beautiful blessing God had bestowed upon me.

Then, I recall the day when I was home alone with my baby for the first time. I was scared out of my wits. "What will I do with her all day?" I asked myself. But the panic gave way to patient acceptance, as I placed my trust in God and His mother Mary. With their unfailing help, I learned to care for my newborn and tried to give her the best possible start in life.

I was shocked when, on her fifth day on earth, she grabbed my cereal bowl as she sat propped up on my lap at the dining room table. I was taken aback by her strength and tenacity but amused, as well. Her adventurous nature brought me joy.

I remember how proud I was a month later, when I dressed my baby for her first big outing — taking in the neighborhood 4th of July parade. With a white bonnet protecting her from the sun, she sat in her infant carrier and watched the passing spectacle. I felt that the holiday celebration was so much sweeter with baby Gabriella by my side.

As a new mother, I had times when my faith in God and my friendship with Mary were tested. After catching a cold one day, Gabriella seemed to be struggling to breathe. Her father and I took her to the hospital emergency room, where the doctor on duty made a preliminary diagnosis of asthma. The physician assessed that she was the sickest young patient there.

I begged God to heal my baby girl. The doctor sent us home with a nebulizer, a medical device that turns liquid medicine into a mist, which the patient inhales.[47] Years of nebulizer treatments followed, but, thankfully, Gabriella was otherwise healthy and even embraced activities such as swimming and ballet with apparent ease.

One of my most joyous moments of motherhood came when my daughter was two-and-a-half years old. She had expressed a love of dance shortly after she learned how to walk, so her father enrolled her in ballet classes. The youngest girl in her class, she seemed to dance to the beat of her own drummer.

This was especially apparent at her recital. While all the other little girls strictly followed the routine their ballet teacher had choreographed for them, Gabriella decided to engage in her own improvisational dance. The audience, assembled in the auditorium, laughed and applauded, and a little star was born. My heart swelled with joy at my daughter's ingenuity and creativity, and it is a memory that I shall always cherish.

Not every woman is called to be a physical mother, but each of us, as women, have a vocation as a spiritual mother. The concept is fairly new to me — again, I do not recall anything in my catechism classes that spoke of spiritual motherhood. But I find it highly comforting, nonetheless.

I know of women who demonstrate their spiritual motherhood by praying for priests. I adopted the practice some time ago, and I have found it to be so comforting, knowing that I am attempting to intercede for those valiant men who bring us the Body and Blood of Christ. Their struggles can be intense, and they may also contend with loneliness and, at times, isolation.

I find immense joy in being able to pray for other people. It is a way in which I can show support, even when I cannot be physically present with them. In social media, the phrase "sending thoughts and prayers" is often maligned. But, in fact, there is no more powerful thing we can do than to lift up our hearts and voices to God in supplication. God hears every prayer, and He will answer us in the time and fashion that is best for us.

I have developed a practice I call "praying through my news feed." I scroll through my Facebook, Twitter, and Instagram feeds and pray a quick "Hail Mary' for all those who are asking for prayer. I then post a quick "praying right now" to let my cyberspace buddy know that prayers are ascending.

When I go to a nearby Adoration chapel, I also take a photo and post it on Facebook, letting my friends know that I am praying for them. Sometimes, they will respond with a specific prayer request, and I am happy to oblige. Prayer-filled posts are a wonderful way to improve the atmosphere on social media, enhancing the amount of kindness on display in between any diatribes you might find.

I have witnessed the power of spiritual motherhood first-hand in the Cursillo movement. During a women's Cursillo weekend, which is similar to a retreat, I have seen women from the age of 17 to their 80s embrace the love of Christ and neighbor in a stirring manner. It is incredible to see the transformations that can arise when women's lives are touched by the love of Jesus and Mary.

I have seen women reaching out to mothers who have suffered great tragedies in their lives, from losing a child in a fatal automobile crash to losing a child to abortion. These women act as the hands and feet of Mary on earth, performing acts of amazing mercy and grace. They serve selflessly, with a determination and strength that are powered by their love for God.

Personal Reflections

1. If you have given birth, did you experience any nervousness as a new mother? How did you manage to cope?

2. To what extent is Mary a role model for you in your motherhood?

3. Has motherhood increased your faith in God? If so, how? If not, what do you perceive as the chief stumbling blocks in your relationship with the Almighty?

4. What actions could you take this week to serve as a spiritual mother to other people?

CHAPTER 10
Encountering Mary
at the Nativity

I recall an Advent season when I was six years old. I was eager to buy a gift for my little sister, one that she would treasure always. My parents had taken us to a department store near our apartment, and I was anxious to make a purchase. We were in a section of the store that had row upon row of shelves featuring various delights. As I reached for what I thought would be the doll of my sister's dreams, a shelf came down on my head with a loud "thud."

My mother informed an associate, and she directed us to a room where I would meet with the department store nurse. As I sat waiting for what seemed like an interminable length of time, I started to cry, thinking that my head injury would cause me to be in the hospital on Christmas Day. The thought of "missing Christmas" made me inconsolable.

I was relieved when the nurse examined me and determined that I would not have to go to the hospital. I walked out of the department store comfortable in the knowledge that I would be celebrating Christmas with the rest of the family.

In the years since, I have come to the realization that nothing can cancel Christmas — that Christ comes to us as a babe in a manger each year, whether we are at home or in the hospital. The Nativity is a powerful statement of Christ's sacrifice, coming to earth in the most vulnerable form possible — that of a baby.

In Luke, Chapter 2, we learn the backdrop of Jesus' appearance on earth:

> In those days a decree went out from Caesar Augustus that the whole world should be enrolled. This was the first enrollment, when Quirinius was governor of Syria. So all went to be enrolled, each to his own town. And Joseph too went up from Galilee from the town of Nazareth to Judea, to the city of David that is called Bethlehem, because he was of the house and family of David, to be enrolled with Mary, his betrothed, who was with child.[48]

Mary and Joseph were faithful citizens, complying with the census, even though the road to obedience included the challenge of preparing for the birth of a child. They respected the state and honored God in all their dealings, giving us an example of how we can function as good citizens and faith-filled servants of the Lord.

It was an arduous journey — all the more so because Mary was about to go into labor.

> While they were there, the time came for her to have her child, and she gave birth to her firstborn son. She wrapped him in swaddling clothes and laid him in a manger, because there was no room for them in the inn.[49]

What a joyful encounter we have with Mary in this Scripture reading! We meet a woman who is incredibly humble, who does not complain when faced with the unexpected, such as no room at the inn. She accepts her circumstances with grace and focuses, as we should, on Christ. This is the type of woman I would like to have as a friend, someone who is willing to sustain hardship in order to bring the very embodiment of Love into the world.

> Now there were shepherds in that region living in the fields and keeping the night watch over their flock. The angel of the Lord appeared to them and the glory of the Lord shone around them, and they were struck with great fear.[50]

We can put ourselves in the place of the shepherds, going about our business, when the miraculous arrives on the scene. How would we respond to an angel in our midst? Fear seems a natural reaction, but it would not be a paralyzing fear; rather, it would be a fear that would give way to faith.

> The angel said to them, "Do not be afraid; for behold, I proclaim to you good news of great joy that will be for all the people. For today in the city of David a savior has been born for you who is Messiah and Lord. And this will be a sign for you: you will find an infant wrapped in swaddling clothes and lying in a manger." And suddenly there was a multitude of the heavenly host with the angel, praising God and saying: "Glory to God in the highest and on earth peace to those on whom his favor rests."[51]

The angel confirms the news that the long-awaited Messiah has been born. The vision includes what must have been a heavenly sound, as the first angel and multitudes of others raised their voices in praise of the Almighty.

> When the angels went away from them to heaven, the shepherds said to one another, "Let us go, then, to Bethlehem to see this thing that has taken place, which the Lord has made known to us." So they went in haste and found Mary and Joseph, and the infant lying in the manger. When they saw

this, they made known the message that had been told them about this child. All who heard it were amazed by what had been told them by the shepherds. And Mary kept all these things, reflecting on them in her heart.[52]

The shepherds have their own joyful encounter with Mary and her Son. It must have been an astonishing sight to be in the presence of the greatness of God's only Son. One can guess that the shepherds were also impressed with Mary, how she had given birth in these challenging circumstances. She is indeed blessed among women.

In giving birth to Jesus, Mary changes the course of history. She is a history-maker *par excellence,* one who plays an unforgettable role in the drama of salvation. Once again, mankind has an opportunity to enjoy paradise, thanks to this amazing woman and her beloved offspring.

It is highly significant that Mary reflects deeply on the arrival of the shepherds, along with the mysterious manner in which her child was born. She does not just think about these occurrences in a passing fashion, but rather contemplates them in the depths of her heart.

In like manner, when we sense the presence of Jesus in our lives, we can meditate upon His arrival with great love and affection. We can pray for wisdom and guidance in assessing what Jesus' intervention in our lives means to us and to our families.

Personal Reflections

1. What can you learn from Mary about faithful citizenship? How can it play a role in your life?

2. Imagine giving birth in a stable and laying your newborn in a manger. What thoughts go through your head?

3. In what ways does the idea of having Mary as a friend appeal to you?

4. How has Jesus shown up in your life this week? What would it mean for you to ponder this appearance in the depths of your heart?

CHAPTER 11
Growing in Virtue:
Poverty in Spirit

I grew up with a father who was loving and gentle, encouraging and creative. As an amateur song-writer, he filled our home with the gift of music. I recall one Christmas where we sat in a department store in a section called SantaLand, waiting for his Christmas song to be played. When I heard the strains of "Randy the Little Elf," his signature song, I cheered.

My father was truly dedicated to his wife and his two children. He was essentially a homebody, and his greatest joy was delighting in the accomplishments of his daughters. He was our cheerleader-in-chief, and we admired him greatly. In many respects, he mirrored the Father in Heaven and, when he passed away, I realized that I had lost one of my best friends.

But my father had great difficulty holding down a job. His unemployment was more regular than his employment. In fact, for the entire time I was in high school, my father did not have a job. We came to rely on my mother as breadwinner, with my Dad's sisters contributing what they could to the care of our household.

To this day, I do not know the specific reason for my father's joblessness, although clinical depression may have played a role. Also, he had dreamed of being a journalist, but, when he was discharged from the military, he ended up studying accounting in college. I often felt as if my father was pursuing the wrong professional path, but he seemed stuck. With no money to go back to school, he continued to apply for accounting jobs. He was hard-working, and at times worked two jobs to support the family. But, for long periods of time, he was a stay-at-home Dad — not by choice, but by necessity.

What I learned from the experience of growing up with such financial insecurity was that God was my ultimate Provider. Since my earthly father had such difficulty providing for our family, I relied on the Almighty to bring us through the tough times. He always did. I was overwhelmed with gratitude for the food that would appear on our table — sometimes bought by relatives, sometimes purchased with food stamps. The fact that we were never homeless — that somehow our rent was paid — seemed equally miraculous.

I experienced a special joy in knowing that God was my Provider. As a child, I knew that He held me in the palm of His Almighty hand. His protection gave me the strength to be diligent in my studies, even when the distractions of our financial difficulties seemed immense. I knew in my heart that I had God to thank for every blessing — even the blessing of being conscientious in my school work. Every good thing in my life originated in God.

Consequently, while our family often survived on quite limited means, I held within my soul a certain joy. It was the joy of knowing that I was profoundly and richly loved by God. I could see God's hand in the arrival of Christmas gifts while my father battled unemployment. I could perceive God's presence in the school uniform that seemed to arrive just in time for the first day of school. I could see God's smile in the grins of my extended family members when they gifted our family with unexpected fruit baskets and other goodies.

The Blessed Mother seemed to find a similar joy in her life. We can all imagine how we would react if our husbands told us there simply wasn't room in the inn. We might scold them for poor planning, or at the very least complain about our lot in life.

But not Mary. She gracefully accepted the cross of giving birth in a stable and laying her Child in a manger. She was among animals, yet she did not raise her voice in complaint. Rather, she accepted her humble circumstances with grace and joy.

A certain freedom accompanies poverty in spirit. When we are not tied to riches … when we give more than we receive … we can experience true freedom and a lightness of being. There is something so liberating about not worrying about personal finances but trusting in God to see us through.

This is not to say that we should abandon those who are hungry and homeless, blithely leaving them to God's care. On the contrary, we have a moral imperative to be, as St. Teresa of Avila noted, the hands and feet of Jesus in the world.[53] We have a duty to reach out to those in dire economic circumstances, sharing with them our blessings. In the eyes of the poor, we can see the reflection of Jesus.

After I grew up, my faith in Christ was severely tested when a downturn in the economy caused me to be laid off from the job I loved. I did not want to apply for unemployment compensation because I thought it would brand me as a failure. But I realized that pride was keeping me from doing what needed to be done, so I filed for benefits.

I had hoped that my period of joblessness would last a few weeks, but, unfortunately, the weeks quickly turned into months. I was touched by the generosity that my friends showed to me, with one even asking if I needed help paying for my meal at a church event. The phrase, "I get by with a little help from my friends," felt so true, and I could really feel the love of Jesus through my friends' generosity. Even though it was a scary time, I experienced the joy of peace, knowing that God was with me and ready and eager to provide for me.

And I can say that God outdid Himself. My employer called me back to work, and once again, I was doing the work that I loved. Never again would I take my job for granted, knowing that bad economic times could cause it to disappear.

Poverty of spirit can be a tough virtue to cultivate in our consumerist society. Advertising is so prevalent that we cannot even log onto social media without being reminded of the latest fashions or the newest electronics. We are inundated with messages to buy, buy, then buy some more. But, as one who becomes obsessed with consumer culture can attest, the desire for more can never be satiated. We cannot find fulfillment in shopping 'til we drop; rather, the hole in our heart can only be filled by God.

We can pray each day for a spirit like Mary's — one that recognizes the generosity of God and tries to emulate it. When we meditate on the Third Joyful Mystery, we can also think about how to show greater abandonment to Divine Providence in our own lives.

Chances are we will never be called to spend the night in a stable among the cows and the donkeys. But we may find we are being called to devote a day to families staying in a homeless shelter or tutoring students from low-income families. In cultivating a spirit of poverty, we can actually richly bless many of the people that cross our path.

Personal Reflections

1. Have you experienced a season of want in your life? What did the experience teach you?

2. Do you see God as your ultimate Provider? Where can you lean on Him in your life?

3. How can you find joy in emulating Mary's poverty of spirit?

4. What action can you take this week to help someone who is in need?

CHAPTER 12
Saintly Encounter:
Saint Juan Diego

Mary, under her title of Our Lady of Guadalupe, is special to me. She is considered a patroness of the pro-life movement, and her image is invoked frequently at peaceful, prayerful pro-life gatherings. Her intercession has been credited with saving the lives of many from the tragedy of abortion.

The relationship between Juan Diego and the Blessed Mother was a true thing of beauty, and it fascinates me. During one of her appearances, she greeted him with the question, *"No estoy yo aqui que soy tu madre?"* which, translated from Spanish to English means, "Am I not here, I who am your mother?"[54] The mother-son relationship is touching and expresses the joy of belonging. Just like Juan Diego, we also belong to Mary, who can provide us with reassurance in the most trying of times.

Born in Mexico in the year 1474, Juan Diego was originally raised as an Aztec pagan. Later, after he had married, he embraced the Catholic religion, under the tutelage of Franciscan missionaries. He was a good and faithful servant of the Lord and was conscientious about his Catholic studies.[55]

He was on his way to church in recognition of the Feast of the Immaculate Conception when he came upon a glorious vision. The woman identified herself as the "mother of the true God."[56] She also communicated to Juan Diego the fact that she was a mother to all mankind.

She dispatched Juan Diego to go to his bishop and tell him that she desired a chapel to be built on Tepeyac Hill, where pagans once worshipped. The bishop was skeptical and asked for time to consider the matter. In the meantime, the Blessed Mother appeared to Juan Diego again, and he informed her about his failure to obtain a commitment from the bishop.

Despite his belief that he was ill-suited for the assignment, Juan Diego subsequently went back to the bishop and asked again that a chapel be built to honor Mary. This time, the bishop told Juan Diego that he needed a sign that Mary's appearance was a real event and not a figment of Juan Diego's imagination. Juan Diego returned to Tepeyac, where he experienced another joyful encounter with the Blessed Mother. Juan Diego relayed to her his conversation with the bishop; in turn, Mary promised to offer him a sign the following day, December 11.

But Juan Diego's uncle became ill, and he felt duty-bound to nurse him back to health. He was en route to locating a priest to minister to his uncle when Mary appeared again before him. She pledged that his uncle would be healed in an effort to relieve his troubled mind. She then directed Juan Diego to go to the hill and pick the flowers he would find there.

Despite the fact that it was December, Juan Diego discovered a multitude of roses, which he placed in his cloak, known as a *tilma*. When Juan Diego went to present the flowers to the bishop, he opened the *tilma* and shocked the bishop with the image embedded in the cloak — an image of Our Lady of Guadalupe.

The miracles continued, as Juan Diego's uncle returned to full health. As Mary had requested, a chapel was built in her honor on Tepeyac Hill. Juan Diego moved into a tiny home on the hill, living a quiet life combining work and prayer. He died on December 9, 1548, and was declared a saint in 2002 under the pontificate of Pope St. John Paul II.[57]

The apparitions are credited with causing the conversion of almost 3,000 indigenous people per day. In recent years, Our Lady of Guadalupe has been cited as a major influence in the lives of people who were once workers in the abortion industry but who subsequently embraced the pro-life cause.

In contemplating Mary's appearances to Juan Diego, our own faith can be strengthened. We can see in Juan Diego the humble servant that we aspire to be. Meanwhile, we can see in Mary the perfect mother for whom we long. She takes us under her mantle and showers us with the love she shared with Jesus.

Personal Reflections

1. What does the message "Am I not here, I who am your mother?" mean to you?

2. How can you demonstrate the faith of Juan Diego this week?

3. Have you, like Juan Diego, felt duty was calling you to one task when the Lord was calling you to something else?

4. This week, see if you can find instances of the Blessed Mother's intervention in your own life.

CHAPTER 13
Loving God's Law

During a period of my childhood, my parents could not afford a car. This meant that our mode of transportation was either the city bus or our own two feet. My mother had a special rule for my sister and me when we were walking on city streets without sidewalks. She even used a little song to help us remember the rule: "Sissy (me) on the inside ... Terri in the middle ... Mommy on the outside. ..." She thought this was the safest way for us to travel, with the adult closest to the traffic.

I knew that the rule was born out of love for us. Our mother was not trying to block our adventures, but rather, she was just trying to ensure that we would be safe on our outing. I realized that my mother was trying to protect us, and I felt safe traveling with her. She was giving us the guardrails along which we could explore the world.

And so it is with God. He puts forward his laws not out of a desire to lord things over us, but to keep us safe and to try to ensure our lasting happiness. When you look at His laws from that perspective, you end up not only growing in love for God but deepening your appreciation for the law itself.

Following God's law can thus lead to an unparalleled joy because, in following God's "rules of the road," we draw closer to Him.

But God does not leave us in a vacuum when it comes to following His law. He also supplies us with His fount of grace to aid us in our obedience through the gift of the Sacraments. As noted by Beginning-Catholic.com, "sacrament" can be defined as "an outward sign instituted by Christ to give grace."[58]

As an outward sign, it is visible and tangible. We think of the bread and wine offered at Mass, which is transformed into the Body and Blood of Christ and shared with us as Holy Communion. We are reminded of the Oil of the Sick used in the Anointing of the Sick when an individual is suffering from grave illness. And we recall the healing waters by which we are baptized as the adopted sons and daughters of God.

I remember vividly the joy that I felt when my youngest cousins were baptized. I thought of how their great-great-grandmother, an immigrant from Italy with little formal education, made sure that her seven children were baptized in the very same church. I gave a quiet thanks to God for the tremendous blessing of Baptism in our family.

My joy was even greater when my own daughter was baptized. I recall the day as one of the happiest times of my life. I had dressed her in an ivory christening gown that enveloped her like a satin blanket. The wisps of strawberry blonde hair that crowned her head captured the light, and she looked for all the world like a pint-sized angel.

I was not sure if this day would ever come. Her godparents were in another state, busy with their own newborn, and could not make the trip to the Baptism. As a result, we had to arrange for a couple we knew in town to serve as proxy godparents. A family friend who was a priest was supposed to fly in for the event, but a storm idled his plane. Thankfully, a priest at the church we attended was willing to do the honors. So, I had approached my daughter's Baptismal day with a great deal of anxiety.

When the water from the baptismal fount was finally poured over her head, I breathed a sigh of relief. She was now an official member of God's family, and I could not have been more joyful. She had been given the incredible gift of sanctifying grace, a share in God's life. She had completed an important rite of passage in our family, and even though she was a baby, she was already a key member of the Kingdom of God.

The experience of my daughter's Baptism made me appreciate all the more the beauty and truth of the Catholic faith. The words ... the symbolism ... the interaction between the elderly priest and the newborn newcomer to the Church ... it all combined to enhance my love of the faith of my fathers. It was one of those "Aha" moments when I realized that I was part of the family of God, and so was my beloved daughter. I could see how the Sacraments bring people together in a community of love.

Loving God's law can be challenging in the secular society in which we live. We are constantly bombarded with messages such as "If it feels good, do it!" and "YOLO," which stands for "You Only Live Once!" Following God's law can seem a lonely enterprise when the culture is preaching a far different gospel.

But the key is to remain steadfast in God's love, which is manifested in His law. We know that God knows what is best for us — and what is not. We can trust Him, knowing that He will never lead us astray. He reveals His law through Sacred Scripture and the tradition of the Church, and we are happiest when we follow it.

In our next chapter, we will see how Mary followed God's law and found joy in the process. May we imitate her in the life of grace.

Personal Reflections

1. Can you recall a rule that your parents or guardians employed in order to keep you safe? How did that rule show their love for you?

2. Are there any laws of God with which you are struggling? Have you tried taking your struggle to prayer?

3. How has your life been enhanced through the Sacrament of Baptism?

4. When have you experienced joy in the Sacraments?

CHAPTER 14
Encountering Mary at the Presentation

In her obedience to God's law, Mary found joy. So, it is not surprising that she would consecrate her Son Jesus to the Lord, in accord with the law that had been handed down by Moses.

The second chapter of Luke informs us of Mary and Joseph's visit with Jesus to the temple when He was still a baby:

> When the days were completed for their purification according to the law of Moses, they took him up to Jerusalem to present him to the Lord, just as it is written in the law of the Lord, "Every male that opens the womb shall be consecrated to the Lord," and to offer the sacrifice of "a pair of turtledoves or two young pigeons," in accordance with the dictate in the law of the Lord.[59]

Now Mary had free will, and she could have easily said to herself, "I don't need to go to the temple." But she was faithful to her Jewish religion and faithful to God, and she followed not only the letter but the spirit of the law.

It is also important to note that God works through people, and Mary's life was about to be touched by the two people she would meet at the temple, Simeon and Anna.

> Now there was a man in Jerusalem whose name was Simeon. This man was righteous and devout, awaiting the consolation of Israel, and the Holy Spirit was upon him. It had been revealed to him by the Holy Spirit that he should not see death before he had seen the Messiah of the Lord."[60]

Simeon had longed to meet the Messiah, the Savior of the world. He was guided by the Holy Spirit and knew in his heart that he would someday see the long-awaited One face-to-face. It was not arrogance that motivated him, but rather simple trust in the Lord.

> He came in the Spirit into the temple; and when the parents brought in the child Jesus to perform the custom of the law in regard to him, he took him into his arms and blessed God, saying: "Now, Master, you may let your servant go in peace, according to your word. ..."[61]

Simeon knew instantly that the baby Jesus was, in fact, the Messiah, despite the humble circumstances of His mother Mary and foster father Joseph.

He gave his thanks to God for bringing him to this incredible moment, recognizing that his life would never be the same. He was at peace, knowing God's word had been fulfilled.

> " … for my eyes have seen your salvation,
> which you prepared in sight of all the peo-
> ples, a light for revelation to the Gentiles,
> and glory for your people Israel."[62]

Simeon recognized Jesus' role in the world: to be God the Father's emissary to the people of Israel. Christ, the Anointed One, was also destined to bring the light of truth to the Gentiles, who lived outside the Jewish faith. Jesus was appointed to be the Savior of all people, the One who would bring about the opening of the gates of paradise.

We learn that Mary and Joseph were "amazed" by what Simeon said. It was just the beginning of many revelations that would come their way. They were raising the boy who would be known as the Son of God. We can surmise that, in their amazement, they felt a profound sense of joy and consolation.

But then came the additional words of Simeon, words that Mary would have to ponder in her heart:

> Simeon blessed them and said to Mary his
> mother, "Behold, this child is destined for
> the fall and rise of many in Israel, and to
> be a sign that will be contradicted (and

you yourself a sword will pierce) so that
the thoughts of many hearts may be
revealed."[63]

Simeon extends to Mary and Joseph a hand
of blessing — he knows he is in the presence of the
individuals who are caring for the King of Kings and
Lord of Lords. He delivers more astonishing words,
indicating that many in Israel will be touched by the
life of Christ. But there is also the cross — a figurative
sword shall pierce Mary's Immaculate Heart. Even
though she is sinless, she will suffer in the days and
years ahead.

And yet, despite the trials and tribulations that
lie before her, Mary can experience joy in the peace
of knowing she is doing God's work. By caring for
the Christ child, she is literally ministering to God
Himself. She can take solace in her pivotal place in
God's plan.

In verses 36-38, we are introduced to Anna, a
prayerful woman who, like Simeon, has been faith-
fully and patiently awaiting the Savior.

There was also a prophetess, Anna, the
daughter of Phanuel, of the tribe of Asher.
She was advanced in years, having lived
seven years with her husband after her
marriage, and then as a widow until she
was eighty-four. She never left the temple,

but worshiped night and day with fasting and prayer. And coming forward at that very time, she gave thanks to God and spoke about the child to all who were awaiting the redemption of Jerusalem.[64]

Anna is graced by the presence of Christ, and she wants to share that experience with everyone she meets. She is convinced, after decades of waiting, that she has laid eyes upon the One who will bring about eternal life for all who believe in Him. Like Simeon, she knows that she can die a happy death, having experienced the revelation of the Lord.

Mary brings joy to Simeon and Anna by bringing Jesus to them. In our own lives, we can also experience the joy of Jesus through Mary, a most devoted mother — not only to Christ, but to all humankind.

Personal Reflections

1. Did this chapter cause you to look upon the Presentation in the Temple with a fresh perspective? How so?

2. When you contemplate the Fourth Mystery of the Rosary, the Presentation, what new insights come to mind?

3. Have you ever waited for a long time — maybe years — for a prayer to be answered? How did that experience affect your faith?

4. In what ways is Mary bringing the joy of Jesus into your life this week?

CHAPTER 15
Growing in Virtue:
Obedience

My mother longed to have more children, but God blessed her with two — a pair of feisty, fiery-tempered girls who challenged her patience on a regular basis. While she wished her brood had been bigger, she realized that corralling her dynamic duo was a daily miracle. As the older child, I accept the blame for the frequent skirmishes between my sister and me.

The fights usually escalated when we were in the back seat of the car. As a result, my father nick-named us "Fuss and Cuss," which caused the two of us to break into an argument over who was who. Two years apart and fiercely competitive, we seldom called a truce.

One incident in particular stands out in my mind. We were en route to an errand dealing with, of all things, my birthday. I was in a particularly cranky mood, and I made my feelings known, loudly and clearly. I was complaining non-stop, and my mother's stress level had reached its limit.

She actually stopped the car to deal with my transgression. I really upset her, and I felt the weight of her pain. It was a breakthrough moment, and my general argumentative episodes came to a thankful end. In that moment, seeing the pain in my mother's eyes, I resolved to be obedient.

I learned a great deal that day — about respect for my parents, respect for my sister, and respect for myself. It was a hard day, but God had brought good out of it. In the midst of suffering, I found a pathway to joy, through obedience.

A couple of years earlier, I had tested my mother through my mendacity. I had been invited to a birthday party by a classmate — a party that was to be held at a roller rink. I had never roller-skated before, and my mother was concerned about my safety. As a result, she decided I was not to attend the party.

But I was undaunted. I lied and told my mother that the roller skating had been canceled, but the party was still on. My mother dropped me off at my classmate's home and went off to do some errands. My classmate's mother then took a group of giggling girls to the roller rink.

While I had a few spills, I managed to escape my skating exploits unscathed. The problem was that my mother returned to my classmate's house earlier than expected, and she figured out that I was at the rink.

My mother was understandably distraught. Not only had I disobeyed her — I had lied in the process. She was greatly disappointed in me.

One day after the incident, we drove to my Grandma Hazel's house. I adored Grandma Hazel and loved spending time at her house, with its swivel chair, rocking chair, and sunlit playroom. As my father used to say, everything was better at Grandma's house.

While we were there, Grandma Hazel invited me to sit in her lap. When I was comfy, she proceeded to explain to me, in a calm and gentle voice, why it was wrong to lie. I burst into tears. I never wanted to disappoint my Grandma Hazel. I couldn't believe the news of my indiscretion had reached her ears. I was beside myself with grief.

I never wanted to hurt my Grandma Hazel again with my lies. As I once heard a priest say, "Nothing good comes from lying." I learned through that experience that the truth, and obedience, would set me free.

I also learned that patience is a virtue because, a few years later, my mother bought me my own pair of skates. She allowed me to whiz through the kitchen, dining room, and living room without a single complaint. Whatever fears she had had about her eldest child on roller skates had disappeared. Perhaps she was also rewarding me for learning my lesson about truth-telling.

As I grew older, I began to question certain aspects of the Catholic faith. Perhaps you have, too. I consumed a great deal of secular media in my training as a broadcast journalist. I began to think that I could remain a Catholic in good standing while rejecting certain tenets of the faith that seemed to be outdated.

For instance, I heard leaders of other denominations who viewed abortion as a "matter of choice." It seemed to me that pregnancy could be quite inconvenient and could seriously derail a woman's educational and professional plans. I bought into the false notion that a "fetus" was not yet a person and therefore not entitled to the full rights guaranteed to persons under the Constitution.

I should also point out that my Sunday Mass attendance was a bit sporadic, and I had abandoned the Sacrament of Reconciliation. A national newspaper was essentially my "Bible," and I only picked up God's Word during Lent. I had little familiarity with the Catechism and paid little heed to the pronouncements of the Pope. In short, I was wandering in a spiritual wilderness and suffering from what I would describe as "spiritual malnutrition."

At that time, I pondered a future that might include running for public office. I recall thinking that, if pressed by the media about my position on abortion, I would respond that "I pray every day for an end to abortion, but I am 'pro-choice.'"

Shortly after this, I met a fellow Catholic who asked me what I was doing to end abortion. I told him I was a journalist, and therefore I could do nothing. He challenged me on that point and loaned me a book written by a pro-life author.

The book opened my eyes to the cruelty of abortion, to ending an innocent human life in the womb. For the first time, I learned about the stages of fetal development. Through my reading, I found out that a heart starts beating 22 days after conception and that brain waves can be detected six weeks following conception.[65] I began to see the humanity of the pre-born child, and I wept at the thought of upwards of a million babies a year dying as a result of "choice."[66]

I vowed to become active in the pro-life movement, attending a monthly Rosary walk to the Planned Parenthood near my church. I became a leader at a church-based Respect Life group and eventually went on to work full-time in the pro-life movement.

I came to realize the beauty and truth of the teachings of the Church and, in trying to abide by them, I felt the joy of profound peace. When I went astray, I could always return to the Sacrament of Reconciliation to right my path.

I have to admit that it took me a while to become re-acclimated to Confession. I had allowed years of sins to build up, like mold on a basement wall. I lacked the courage and fortitude to confess my sins to a priest and fell for the false notion that Reconciliation wasn't necessary in my life. I would say a quick "I'm sorry" to God for my transgressions, without taking advantage of the graces the Sacrament of Reconciliation provides.

I happened to notice an announcement in the bulletin of my parents' parish, offering a one-day retreat. On a whim, I decided to sign up. The retreat proved to be a turning point in my life and in my relationship with God. I summoned up the courage to go to Confession for the first time in years. While I wondered if the priest would remember the sins of the "girl in the pink coat," I felt the joy of surrendering to God. It transformed my life, and I experienced a renewed interest in prayer.

Through daily recitation of the Rosary, I opened a dialogue with Mary. I began to turn to her outside of my Rosary time, just to chat. I poured my heart out to her. I presented her with the various "knots" in my life and asked her to untie them. I placed my worries in her immaculate hands and pleaded with her to take them to the Father to deal with them. In my prayers for Mary's intercession, I found lasting joy.

Perhaps you have struggled with Church teaching, as well. With so much of our modern culture and media railing against the truths that the Catholic Church teaches, living a life faithful to the Church can seem daunting. Know that you have a friend in Mary. Confide in her with your questions and concerns. Ask her for her intercession with God to give you an understanding heart, especially where Church teachings are concerned. Ask God for the grace to model Mary in your obedience to Him.

I have experienced first-hand the tremendous changes that can occur in a soul that is willing to be open to what the Church has to say about the critical issues of our time. Follow Mary's lead to "do whatever he tells you" and you will experience unparalleled joy.

Personal Reflections

1. Were there certain rules that you struggled to obey when you were a child?

2. Have you ever felt God's loving correction when you disobeyed one of His laws? Have you held onto the conviction that He continues to love you, no matter what your transgressions?

3. As an adult, are there certain Church teachings with which you struggle? Would you be willing to take your concerns to Mary?

4. Can you recall an incident in which you found joy in obedience? What did the incident teach you?

CHAPTER 16
Saintly Encounter:
Saint Thérèse of Lisieux

A legacy of love flows through my family for St. Thérèse of Lisieux. It began with my mother, who kept a picture of the valiant young saint on her nightstand. She had had the picture since she was a young girl, trying to deal with the aftermath of her family falling apart. My mother knew that, in her pain, she could call on St. Thérèse for intercession. It made her young life more manageable, and her devotion to "The Little Flower" continued to her dying day.

As an adult, I began a perpetual novena for the intercession of St. Thérèse. The prayer has helped me cope in the toughest of times, and I am always grateful for the roses St. Thérèse sends — sometimes literal, sometimes figurative — that beautify my path. On days of great difficulty, St. Thérèse remains a go-to saint for me — one to whom I turn again and again in the hope of attaining peace of mind.

When my daughter was very young, I showed her a film about St. Thérèse. By the end of the movie, little Gabriella was weeping. She looked around the room and moved toward the crucifix, then proceeded to touch the base of it with her hand. It was as if she knew that St. Thérèse was showing her the way toward God, and she had to embrace the moment.

Although she lived in the 19th century, St. Thérèse's "Little Way" of holiness — offering up the daily trials and tribulations of life for the sake of God's Kingdom — continues to hold popular appeal.

Born in 1873 in France, Thérèse suffered a terrible blow when she was only four-and-a-half years old when her mother died of cancer.[67] She developed an especially tight bond with her older sister Pauline, making it an especially painful experience when Pauline left home to become a Carmelite nun.

Thérèse became despondent and quite ill — so ill that her family feared she would die from her high fever. Desperate for some relief, Thérèse and her sisters prayed to the Blessed Mother. The statue of Mary in Thérèse's room seemed to smile at Thérèse — a miracle that led to her healing. In this way, in the midst of a terrible ordeal, Thérèse had her own joyful encounter with Mary as Our Lady of the Smile.

On the subject of joy, Thérèse once said, "I learned from experience that joy does not reside in the things about us, but in the very depths of the soul, that one can have it in the gloom of a dungeon as well as in the palace of a king."[68]

Given her special relationship with the Blessed Virgin Mary, it is altogether fitting that Thérèse would experience another miracle at Christmastime, when she was 14 years old.[69] An overly sensitive child, she was prone to burst into tears at the slightest provocation. As a result, her sister Celine braced for Thérèse to have an emotional meltdown when they heard her father lamenting about the childhood custom of having gifts placed in their shoes each Christmas.

But her father's comment led to a conversion of heart for Thérèse. She did not cry; rather, she gratefully accepted the gifts as if nothing had happened. Thérèse knew it was the love of Mary's Son, Jesus, which rescued her from her emotionally manipulative ways.

This conversation led to a new sense of charity for Thérèse. As Thérèse once said, "True charity consists in bearing all our neighbour's defects — not being surprised at their weakness, but edified at their smallest virtues."[70]

Thérèse desperately wanted to follow her sisters Pauline, Marie, and Leonie into religious life, but was considered too young for the convent. Undeterred, she took her plea to the Holy Father in Rome. Her appeal was so relentless that security guards had to carry her away from the Holy Father.[71]

Eventually Thérèse did realize her dream of entering Carmel, pursuing a humble life of sacrifice. Much like the Blessed Mother, Thérèse's work was hidden from public view, her sacrifices known to God alone. After their father's death, Celine joined the convent, sparking a new sense of joy in Thérèse.

Her sister Pauline instructed her to record her memories in a journal that would form the basis of the best-selling book *Story of a Soul.*[72] While she died at the tender age of 24, Thérèse's influence became world-renowned. Her undying devotion to both Mary and Jesus made her a role model for generations of young women.

I have read *Story of a Soul* a number of times and, each time, I gain additional insights. The beauty of Thérèse's soul captures my heart, and I long to have her abundant faith. It is no wonder that she has been named a Doctor of the Church because her writings reflect the eloquence of the feminine genius.

Thérèse found the secret of joy in serving others and responding to insults and injuries with a beatific smile. As she wrote, "When something painful or disagreeable happens to me, instead of a melancholy look, I answer by a smile. At first I did not always succeed, but now it has become a habit which [sic] I am glad to have acquired."[73]

Her cheery outlook helped her to weather the challenges that appeared in her life. It was not an unrealistic, heavily saccharine point of view, but rather an attitude built upon a solid faith. Her determination to let roses fall from Heaven after her death demonstrates the depth of her love for other people — a love she had seen in the life of the Blessed Mother. Separated from a mother's love early in life as a result of the death of her earthly mother, she clung to Mary like a toddler at her mother's knee.

Personal Reflections

1. What have you learned from St. Thérèse that you can apply to your life?

2. Have you experienced a conversion of heart, similar to St. Thérèse's? If not, what do you think is blocking your spiritual progress?

3. Have you ever found joy, like the Blessed Mother and St. Thérèse, in performing the humbling tasks of your vocation?

4. Make a list of what would be the highlights of the story of your own soul. What stands out to you?

CHAPTER 17
Finding the Missing

One of my earliest memories is when I was a toddler, spending time at an amusement park in the state in which we lived. My sister, mother, father, and I were accompanied by my paternal grandmother, whom I called Grandma.

Grandma decided to take me to the merry-go-around — an experience I absolutely adored. The problem was that we became separated from my parents and my baby sister, and they did not know where I was. My parents were naturally panicked and began a frantic search. Thankfully, the search ended in our happy reunification. And I learned an important lesson about making sure I checked with my mother and father before attempting a ride on a carousel.

Fast forward a few years, and it was my sister's turn to learn a lesson. We were out on a shopping trip with my mother's foster mother — my Grandma Hazel — at a local department store. While my mother and Grandma Hazel were rifling through the racks, my two-year-old sister wandered off. When my mother discovered that my sister was no longer with us, she asked me if I knew where she was. "Maybe she's been kidnapped," I said. My preschool brain reached for the worst possible scenario, heightening my mother's anxiety.

My mother enlisted a store associate to begin the search for my baby sister. It ended in a dressing room, where the associate found my sister napping. My mother's joy at finding her lost child was inexplicable and is forever etched in my mind.

Fast forward again, and now I have a child of my own — a lovely fair-haired daughter who has brought immeasurable love into my life. My marriage to her father had ended and been annulled by the Church, and I was undergoing custody proceedings.

One Labor Day weekend, on a trip to the local shopping mall, I spotted a huge banner with a lovely picture of a red-headed newborn baby. It was only a few dollars, but I thought it would make quite an impression in my office at work.

So, that weekend, I took to decorating. In addition to the banner, I also hung a number of the awards I had received during my time as a journalist. I felt like making a statement: that, despite the heartache I was experiencing with Gabriella's absence, my life had value and meaning. Through the grace of God, I had accomplished a great deal in my professional life, and it was time for me to recognize those accomplishments.

After I finished my interior design session, I drove to my local community center. It was a lovely weekend, with sunshine pouring down onto the park adjacent to the gym. There was also a wooded section next to the park, with a trail that hikers could traverse. I decided that this was a glorious day for a walk, and I decided to cap off my gym workout with a hike.

As happy as I felt enjoying that last blast of summer, I recognized in my heart that something — or rather, someone — was missing: my child. I decided I wanted to share this experience with her, if only via telephone.

I pulled out my cellphone and called her father's number. The call went to voicemail, and I left a message for my daughter. I had tried to call her earlier that weekend, and I had gotten her father's voice mail then, too. I thought it was strange that I was unable to reach her.

I had made it a habit to not allow two days to go by without calling my mother. Since she and my father were getting older, I felt I needed to check up on them. Besides that, I just enjoyed talking to my mother. She was so supportive of me and had a knack for giving me words of comfort during diffi-cult moments.

This call was no different. I let her know that I had not been able to reach Gabriella the entire weekend.

"You need to call her school and find out if she's been there," my mother advised.

I did have a sinking feeling that something was amiss, so I called the school later that week. The principal informed me that she had not been there in days. He told me that the school had had an inquiry about her from another school in Ontario. "Canada?" I asked. He said he did not know.

I now had a missing child.

For a frantic two weeks, I made phone calls and searched the internet. Someone had given me a prayer journal, and I began writing in it each day, hoping that God and Mother Mary would somehow lead me to her.

As I was agonizing over my daughter's whereabouts, I read this line in my journal: "How can we come to know the peace and rest that exist in conversing with our Father if we do not grasp that He is in control of all things?" In one entry, I wrote in response: "I know that I can be at peace, realizing that He is in control. I don't need to try to wrestle that control away — my arms are too short to box with God." On September 15th of that year, I wrote, "Prayer answered. Gabriella found safe at St. Anne's school, Peterborough, Ontario. Praise God — the Almighty, the all-powerful, the all-loving."[74]

Thanks to God and Google, I had finally located Gabriella in Canada. My joy was overflowing, as was my gratitude. And, in that moment of discovery, I felt as if I had experienced a taste of what Mary had when she found her Son Jesus in the temple.

I hope you never have to experience the agony of having a missing child. But perhaps you've lost something in your life — a sense of hope, an important relationship, a job. Maybe you are yearning for the recovery of that thing that has been lost, that precious jewel that you prized so much.

Please know that Mary stands ever present to console you, to wrap her mantle around your shoulders during this difficult time. She cares for you, just as her heart went out to her Son at Calvary. She is fully prepared to shoulder your burden with you and pray for the strength you need to carry your cross.

Whatever your struggle is, you can find joy in the knowledge that the God Who brought Mary into the world loves you with an everlasting love. Pray for Mary's sweet intercession that God will help you find joy again.

Personal Reflections

1. Have you felt lost at various points in your life? Looking back, can you see that God was right with you during those times of difficulty?

2. Are you healing from a relationship that has been lost? How do you think Mary can help you during this time?

3. Have you ever experienced joy at finding something (or someone) that was lost? Take a few moments to praise God for that moment of bliss.

4. Are you struggling to find your joy again? Meditate on the revelations found in the Fifth Joyful Mystery of the Rosary. How do you think God is working in your life amidst your struggle?

CHAPTER 18

Encountering Mary at the Finding of Jesus in the Temple

The Fifth Joyful Mystery makes my heart glad. The thought of the happy reunion between mother and child always moved me — even before I had experienced the trauma of having a missing child.

To fully understand the depth of the mystery, let's examine the scriptural basis for it: Luke 2:41-52. The passage begins:

> Each year his parents went to Jerusalem for the feast of Passover, and when he was twelve years old, they went up according to festival custom.[75]

Again, we see Mary's obedience at work. She and Joseph commemorate the Passover in keeping with Jewish law. It takes some effort on their part, traveling to Jerusalem, but they are willing to take on any hardships that might come their way.

> After they had completed its days, as they were returning, the boy Jesus remained behind in Jerusalem, but his parents did not know it. Thinking that he was in the caravan, they journeyed for a day and

looked for him among their relatives and acquaintances, but not finding him, they returned to Jerusalem to look for him.[76]

What a shock it must have been for Mary and Joseph to discover that the beloved Jesus was missing. Here, they had been entrusted with the Savior of the world, and they had lost sight of Him. Their emotional pain must have been intense. This was the boy Mary had birthed, nursed, and raised — she had been ever at his side during his first twelve years of life. To lose track of him had to have been a devastating blow.

We have to keep in mind that, while sinless, Mary was human, and she would experience all the emotions that the mother of a missing child would: fear, anger, frustration. The tidal wave of emotions would have been difficult to bear. And yet, she was filled with grace — God's life within her — and she was equipped to shoulder this cross.

After three days they found him in the temple, sitting in the midst of the teachers, listening to them and asking them questions, and all who heard him were astounded at his understanding and his answers.[77]

Imagine Mary's face when she laid eyes on Jesus after a tense three-day search for Him — to know that

He was safe from harm and, what's more, was in the company of learned teachers who were "astounded" by His responses in what must have been a memorable verbal exchange. The joy in her heart must have been overflowing after finding her Son.

But then, good Mother that she was, Mary asked for an explanation.

> "Son, why have you done this to us? Your father and I have been looking for you with great anxiety."[78]

Mary's bewilderment must have been evident. Why had her Son gone off on his own? Knowing that He would be causing Mary and Joseph such anguish, *why* did he do it?

Jesus' reply might catch us off guard, but it is indicative of who He is and what He was meant to accomplish on earth.

> And he said to them, "Why were you looking for me? Did you not know that I must be in my Father's house?"[79]

But Mary and Joseph did not understand. They were like any parents who had lived the nightmare of having a missing child. The entire experience mystified them.

Isn't it true of us, as well, that we can be totally perplexed by the ways of God? When troubles arise, we may search for Him and have difficulty finding Him in the midst of our sadness. But the story does not end there — neither for Mary nor for us.

> He went down with them and came to Nazareth, and was obedient to them; and his mother kept all these things in her heart.[80]

Mary models for us true discipleship: she remains committed to Christ, even when His ways seem mysterious. She ponders the circumstances of Jesus' disappearance and reappearance, knowing that the Lord works in ways that routinely test our faith. We need to remain open to Jesus and His saving message in all circumstances and in all times, even when it is difficult.

Sometimes, we need to wait in order to see the fruition of God's plan in our lives. As the following verse shows, Jesus grew to become the Man the Father intended.

> And Jesus advanced [in] wisdom and age and favor before God and man.[81]

Personal Reflections

1. Have you been searching for Jesus amidst the troubles in your life?

2. Where can you see the hand of God working through your life this week?

3. To what extent does the saying, "The Lord works in mysterious ways," apply to your life?

4. How can you maintain your joy during times of uncertainty?

CHAPTER 19
Growing in Virtue: Joy in Finding Jesus

So many times I have focused on the anxiety that Mary felt at having lost Jesus. But how much more I should ponder the joy that the Blessed Mother experienced in finding Jesus? I believe it is this joy that the Lord wishes for each of us. Not a momentary spark of happiness, but a lasting joy that no amount of trouble can erase.

I am reminded of the words of an old hymn: "Jesus my Lord, my God, my All! How can I love Thee as I ought?"[82] For it is in loving Jesus that we find joy. But sometimes the gateway to loving Jesus is loving His mother.

I recall when I was a little girl. I couldn't wait to run up to and hug my mother. Placing my arms around her waist was the best feeling in the world. I knew that she loved me with a fierce and vibrant love, and I wanted to return that love to her.

Since I had no money with which to shower her with gifts, I would race out to the backyard and pick pansies for her. I would carefully arrange them into a bouquet and present them to her as if she had just been crowned Mrs. America. I took the riches that I found in our garden and bestowed them on her as my queen. And, in that precious moment, I also felt the love of Jesus.

A few years later, I found Jesus in a whole new, exciting way — through my reception of Holy Communion. This was the tangible Jesus in the guise of bread and wine. My First Communion made my heart dance and filled me with a love I had not known before. I had, by this time, already developed a devotion to Mary, and that relationship led me to her son. The amazing thing is that I can find this joy again, over and over again, through frequent reception of Holy Communion. When I am unable to get to Mass, I can experience a Spiritual Communion by simply asking Jesus into my heart. During times of suffering, I can still find joy through Communion with Christ.

As a youngster, I also found the joy of Jesus through the Sacrament of Reconciliation. My first experience with Confession occurred on the afternoon of Christmas Eve. While I had some trepidation at the thought of confessing my sins to a priest, I knew that I was really confessing my transgressions to Jesus, with the priest acting in his stead. I felt as if my soul gleamed after the priest offered absolution. That night, I was scheduled to sing with the rest of the children's choir at Midnight Mass. I couldn't wait to tell my classmates about my newfound joy after receiving God's forgiveness.

I am so fortunate that the Sacrament of Reconciliation is available each week at my parish. I can experience the joy of my personal slate being wiped clean repeatedly. If you have not been to Confession in a while, I highly recommend it for increasing your joy quotient. There is nothing quite like a clear conscience for helping one find peace. Again, I believe it has been my relationship with Mary that has helped me to seek out the Sacrament of Reconciliation to heal my troubled heart.

Mary has also led me to a commitment for weekly Adoration of the Blessed Sacrament. I am fortunate to have a 24-hour Adoration chapel located in the city in which I live. If you do not have an Adoration chapel nearby, check to see if your parish offers hours of Adoration on a weekly or monthly basis. From my own experience, I can tell you that Adoration can change your life. To be in the presence of the exposed Host — to feel the love of Jesus pouring forth — is a powerful experience.

At Adoration, I present to Jesus a list of pressing prayer intentions, confident that He will answer me in some way. I also place in His sacred hands my worries and frustrations, knowing that He is ever ready to guide me in times of uncertainty.

Saint Teresa of Calcutta once said, "When you look at the crucifix, you understand how much Jesus loved you then. When you look at the Sacred Host, you understand how much Jesus loves you now."[83]

Indeed, time spent in Adoration can feel as if we are experiencing Heaven on earth. As St. Thérèse of Lisieux said, "Heaven for me is hidden in a little Host Where Jesus, my Spouse, is veiled for love. I go to that Divine Furnace to draw out life, and there my sweet Saviour listens to me night and day."[84]

Some people are perplexed as to what to do in Adoration. They worry they will grow bored sitting before the Sacred Host for an hour. Saint Teresa of Avila recommended bringing a book along to prompt meditation and prayer. Just pouring out your heart to God can be a soul-cleansing experience.

We can also take advice from St. Clare of Assisi, who stated, "Gaze upon him, consider him, contemplate him, as you desire to imitate him."[85]

While the feeling of being in the physical presence of the Body and Blood of Christ is unparalleled, you can also access a livestream of Adoration chapels around the world with the help of the internet. When the Coronavirus pandemic began, our local Adoration chapel was closed to the public. So, I found spiritual sustenance viewing Adoration chapels online. Adoration can yield great spiritual fruit in our lives. Saint Peter of Alcántara pointed out, "Our Lord in the Blessed Sacrament has His hands full of graces, and He is ready to bestow them on anyone who asks for them."[86]

We can also find Jesus in other people. I have experienced great joy on Cursillo weekends, where I have joined a team of women in sharing the love of Christ with newcomers to the movement. Sharing one's faith can be a joy-filled journey — one I highly recommend. A spiritual retreat, whether at a retreat house or at your own parish, can also energize your faith.

Recall that it was a retreat at my parents' parish that led me to return to the Sacrament of Reconciliation after a long absence. At the retreat, I experienced my own personal *metanoia*, a change of heart that inspired me to embrace that which scared me — a meeting with a priest in the confessional. You may find a retreat similarly soul-stirring, helping you to enhance your relationships with both Mary and Jesus.

Many of my friends and I have found joy and fellowship through weekly study programs offered by our parish. These include Bible study, study of the *Catechism*, and the *Women of Grace* foundational study. Studies are a marvelous way to connect with fellow parishioners, to make friends, and to grow in love of Jesus.

When we make a valiant effort to search for Jesus, we may find that some of our friends are mystified by our quest. At times, these individuals may even abandon us, not understanding what a friend they could have in Jesus. That is why it is all the more important to seek out Christian fellowship. Some may dismiss your newfound friends as "church ladies," but I have found that a group of faith-filled women can be a powerful antidote against loneliness and despair.

Personal Reflections

1. Do you recall your First Holy Communion? How can you recapture that joy through frequent reception of Communion in your life today?

2. In what ways can frequent visits to the confessional bring you joy?

3. If you were at Adoration right now, what would you say to God?

4. Is there a study at your parish in which you can participate? What, if anything, is holding you back?

CHAPTER 20
Saintly Encounter:
Saint Gianna Molla

When looking for a saintly example from my own family tree, I am often reminded of the woman I called "Grandma." My father's mother was an immigrant from Italy who came to the United States when she was about five years old. She married very young and had seven children, whom she loved as if each was her one and only. Grandma and Grandpa weathered wicked financial storms, raising their brood on the modest salary Grandpa earned as a barber.

Despite her financial difficulties, Grandma was exceedingly generous, regularly sharing baked goods with her neighbors. She could only afford to serve meat to her family once a week, but she was an incredible cook, doing the best she could with what the good God gave her. She was a model of patience and humility, working around the clock to meet the needs of her family. There was no one quite like her, and, in my best moments, I attempt to emulate her quiet courage and strength.

Because of my Grandma's Italian roots, I tend to think of her when I hear about St. Gianna Beretta

Molla, who was born in Magenta, Italy in 1922.[87] Like my Grandma, Gianna was devoted to faith and family, and her life revolved around the Church. But Gianna differed from my paternal grandmother in that she worked outside the home, as a pediatrician.

In 1954, Gianna met the love of her life, Pietro Molla, and the next year, the happy couple married.[88] Gianna was a pro at balancing her professional life with her personal life, giving birth to three children in quick succession: Pierluigi, Maria Zita, and Laura. As Gianna once said, "One earns Paradise with one's daily task."[89]

As a mother, Gianna had a special relationship with the Blessed Virgin Mary and drew strength and sustenance from their common bond.

The following reflection demonstrates the love Gianna had for the Blessed Mother:

> O Mary, into your maternal hands I place myself and I abandon myself completely, sure of obtaining whatever I ask of you. I trust in you because you are the sweet Mother, I confide in you because you are the Mother of Jesus. In this trust I place myself, sure of being heard in everything; with this trust in my heart I greet you "my Mother, my trust," I devote myself entirely to you, begging you to remember that I am yours, that I belong to you; keep

me and defend me, O sweet Mary, and in every instant of my life, present me to your Son, Jesus.[90]

In her life outside the home, Gianna was especially drawn to assisting the most vulnerable, including the poor and disenfranchised. She had a generous heart for those who were suffering and needed additional care.

Gianna experienced much joy in her life, as evidenced by this quote: "The secret of happiness is to live moment by moment and to thank God for all that He, in His goodness, sends to us day after day."[91]

The test of Gianna's love came during her pregnancy with her fourth child. When Gianna began experiencing intractable pain, doctors discovered that she had a tumor in her uterus. They offered her the option of abortion, but Gianna refused, choosing instead to have the tumor removed while safeguarding her preborn child's life. Her daughter Gianna Emanuela was born in April 1962, but sadly Gianna lost her personal battle for life one week after her baby's birth, dying from septic peritonitis.[92]

Pope St. John Paul II canonized Gianna in May 2004, with her husband and children present at the canonization. It marked the first time a husband had been present for his wife's declaration of sainthood. Saint Gianna is considered to be a special patron of mothers, pre-born babies, and the pro-life movement.

Gianna's belief in the connection between love and sacrifice can be seen in this quote: "Love and sacrifice are closely linked, like the sun and the light. We cannot love without suffering and we cannot suffer without love."[93]

I find Gianna is a saint to whom I can really relate on a woman-to-woman level. After all, this was a woman who loved to pore through fashion magazines and seemed to revel in the blessings of modern life. Yet, she possessed a holiness that was truly attractive. She was a true conduit for the love of Jesus and Mary and showered that love on her husband, her children, and her patients.

She paid the ultimate price for her motherhood, giving up her very life for her child. What an incredible witness for the sanctity of life! What a wonderful role model, not only for this generation of women, but for generations hence!

Personal Reflections

1. Can you relate to St. Gianna Molla in her quest to serve both family and community?

2. As a mother (either physical or spiritual), how are you being called to sacrifice for those in your care?

3. What can you learn from Gianna's relationship with Mary?

4. How might you be called to give of yourself to protect the sanctity of precious human life?

CONCLUSION
Next Steps in Your Walk with Mary

$\maltese$

As I hope you have experienced in these pages, walking hand-in-hand with Mary can be a joyful adventure. She radiates the love of Christ and, in turn, helps us to have a more meaningful relationship with her beloved Son.

We may often say to our friends, "I'm only a text message away." Mary is even closer to our hearts, ready to meet us where we are, in the midst of our struggles. Her beauty shines forth in a way that can make our hearts dance, even amidst the difficulties of life.

I do not mean to suggest that life is an endless joy ride. Trauma and tragedy can be found around the next bend. But, if we share our emotional pain with Mary, we can find it easier to endure for the long haul.

Keep in mind the words of St. Teresa of Avila, a Doctor of the Church: "We always find that those who walked closest to Christ were those who had to bear the greatest trials."[94]

Crosses are naturally going to come our way. The question is: How will we respond to them? I hope I will respond as Mary did, with grace and perseverance, pondering all things in her heart.

By contemplating the Joyful Mysteries and how they relate to our lives, we can grow in the joy of Jesus, who is the Bridge to our ultimate happiness. We reflect on the way God weaved a tapestry of hope in the lives of Mary and Jesus, through the Annunciation, the Visitation, the Nativity, the Presentation, and the Finding of the Lord Jesus in the Temple. That hope can bear good fruit in our own lives.

If you find it difficult to pray the Rosary on your own, I recommend that you find someone with whom you can share the experience. It could be a family member, a friend, or fellow parishioners. My Cursillo group uses videoconferencing to pray the Rosary on our laptops, iPads, and iPhones, and we have found it to be an incredible bonding experience, especially during the isolation created amidst the COVID-19 pandemic.

Here are a few more tips for you as you begin (or continue) your walk with Mary:

- Begin each day by offering your time, troubles, joys, and hopes to Mary. I have found this prayer to be especially helpful: "Blessed Virgin Mary, I offer you all my prayers, works, and sacrifices this day in reparation for my sins and those of the whole world."

- Spend some time each week in a heart-to-heart talk with Mary. Bring your struggles to her, and ask her to untie the knots in your life.

- Consider praying a novena (nine days of prayer) to Mary, under her title of Our Lady of Lourdes or Our Lady of Fátima (You can find these in the iPhone app called "Laudate," or Google them online.).

- Make a 54-day Rosary Novena to Our Lady (You can discover details of this powerful prayer online).

- Consecrate yourself to the Immaculate Heart of Mary, using a resource such as the fabulous book *33 Days to Morning Glory* by Fr. Michael Gaitley, MIC. In the consecration, you will offer all your good works and sufferings, along with your prayers, to the Blessed Mother in a tremendous example of self-giving. I guarantee you, after your consecration, your life will never be the same.

Many of us may feel a bit shell-shocked because of the troubles in our world — everything from public health crises to violence in our streets. In the midst of all of this devastating news, it can be heartening to reflect on the Gospel message, as illustrated through the Joyful Mysteries of the Rosary. We can rest in the knowledge that God is in control amid the strife in our communities and in our country.

When I consecrated myself to the Immaculate Heart of Mary, I had no idea what would await me: the thrill of pregnancy, the amazing birth of a lovely daughter, a full-time calling to the pro-life movement. In the words of a classic Hollywood film, it continues to be a "Wonderful Life." Even amid traumas such as marital breakdown and a missing child, God has remained faithful — and Mary has pointed the way to Him.

I can feel safe and secure, knowing that Mary and Jesus are with me, every step of the way. I pray that you, too, will experience a *Journey of Joy* that will last a lifetime.

Personal Reflections

1. What joys have you experienced since reading this book?

2. In what ways do the mysteries of the Holy Rosary apply to your life this week?

3. Despite your crosses, in what ways have you found your life to be a "Wonderful Life?"

4. How has Mary manifested herself in your life this week?

Additional Rosary Resources

ARTICLES

"The Fruits of the Mysteries of the Rosary," Patrice Fagnant MacArthur, Catholic Exchange, catholicexchange.com/fruits-mysteries-of-the-rosary.

"A Scriptural Reflection on the Rosary," Maryann Marshall, EWTN, www.ewtn.com/catholicism/library/scriptural-reflection- on-the-rosary-11847.

"How to Pray the Rosary," Marians of the Immaculate Conception, www.marian.org/mary/rosary/howto.php.

"My Rosary Story: My Mother's LifeLine Became Mine," Maria V. Gallagher, CatholicMom.com, www.catholicmom.com/articles/my-rosary-story-my-mothers-lifeline-became-mine.

"The Mysteries of the Rosary," The Vatican, www.vatican.va/special/rosary/documents/misteri_en.html.

BOOKS

Benkovic, Johnette S. *The Rosary: Your Weapon for Spiritual Warfare*. Servant Books: 2017.

Calloway, Donald H. *Champions of the Rosary*, Marian Press: 2016.

Crowe, Gretchen. *Why the Rosary, Why Now?* Our Sunday Visitor: 2017.

De Monfort, St. Louis-Marie. *The Secret of the Rosary*, Martino Fine Books: 2018.

Gaitley, Michael E. *33 Days to Morning Glory*, Marian Press: 2011.

Ilibagiza, Immaculée with Erwin, Steve. *The Rosary: The Prayer That Saved My Life*. Hay House, Inc.: 2014.

Longenecker, Fr. Dwight. *Praying the Rosary for Inner Healing*, Our Sunday Visitor: 2008.

Sri, Edward. *Praying the Rosary Like Never Before: Encounter the Wonder of Heaven and Earth,* Franciscan Media: 2017.

PODCASTS

"Girlfriends (A Podcast for Catholic Women)," Danielle Bean, girlfriends.fireside.fm/tags/the%20family%20rosary.

"Pray the Rosary with Bishop Barres," Podbean, www.podbean.com/podcast-detail/c6htg-360d4/Pray-the-Rosary-with-Bishop-Barres-Podcast.

"Rosary Podcasts," Archdiocese of Louisville, www.archlou.org/about-the-archdiocese/publications-media/rosary-podcasts.

"Unlocking the Power of the Rosary," Crossroads Initiative, www.crossroadsinitiative.com/media/podcasts/unlocking-the-power-of-the-rosary-podcast.

VIDEOS

"Holy Rosary in Time of Pandemic," EWTN, www.youtube.com/watch?v=MFQ1B-9v-c8.

"The Rosary," Catholic TV, www.catholictv.org/shows/the-rosary.

"The Rosary in Two Minutes," Busted Halo, bustedhalo.com/video/the-rosary-in-two-minutes.

"The Traditional Catholic Rosary," Formed, watch.formed.org/videos/the-traditional-catholic-rosary.

"Explaining the Faith: The Rosary, Parts 1 and 2," Fr. Chris Alar, MIC: youtube.com/c/DivineMercy_Official.

Morning Glory Consecration Prayer
from *33 Days to Morning Glory*
by Fr. Michael Gaitley, MIC.

I, _____, a repentant sinner, renew and ratify today in your hands, O Immaculate Mother, the vows of my Baptism. I renounce Satan and resolve to follow Jesus Christ even more closely than before.

Mary, I give you my heart. Please set it on fire with love for Jesus. Make it always attentive to His burning thirst for love and for souls. Keep my heart in your most pure Heart that I may love Jesus and the members of His Body with your own perfect love.

Mary, I entrust myself totally to you: my body and soul, my goods, both interior and exterior, and even the value of all my good actions. Please make of me, of all that I am and have, whatever most pleases you.

Let me be a fit instrument in your immaculate and merciful hands for bringing the greatest possible glory to God. If I fall, please lead me back to Jesus. Wash me in the blood and water that flow from His pierced side, and help me never to lose my trust in this fountain of love and mercy. With you, O Immaculate Mother — you who always do the will of God — I unite myself to the perfect consecration of Jesus as He offers Himself in the Spirit to the Father for the life of the world. Amen.

Litany of Humility

By Cardinal Rafael Merry del Val y Zulueta (1865-1930)

O Jesus, meek and humble of heart,

Hear me.

From the desire of being esteemed,

Deliver me, O Jesus.

From the desire of being loved,

Deliver me, O Jesus.

From the desire of being extolled,

Deliver me, O Jesus.

From the desire of being honored,

Deliver me, O Jesus.

From the desire of being praised,

Deliver me, O Jesus.

From the desire of being preferred to others,

Deliver me, O Jesus.

From the desire of being consulted,

Deliver me, O Jesus.

From the desire of being approved,

Deliver me, O Jesus.

From the fear of being humiliated,

Deliver me, O Jesus.

From the fear of being despised,

Deliver me, O Jesus.

From the fear of suffering rebukes,

Deliver me, O Jesus.

From the fear of being calumniated,

Deliver me, O Jesus.

From the fear of being forgotten,

Deliver me, O Jesus.

From the fear of being ridiculed,

Deliver me, O Jesus.

From the fear of being wronged,

Deliver me, O Jesus.

From the fear of being suspected,

Deliver me, O Jesus.

That others may be loved more than I,

Jesus, grant me the grace to desire it.

That others may be esteemed more than I,

Jesus, grant me the grace to desire it.

That, in the opinion of the world,
others may increase and I may decrease,

Jesus, grant me the grace to desire it.

That others may be chosen and I set aside,

Jesus, grant me the grace to desire it.

That others may be praised and I go unnoticed,

Jesus, grant me the grace to desire it.

That others may be preferred to me in
everything,

Jesus, grant me the grace to desire it.

That others may become holier than I,
provided that I may become as holy as I should,

Jesus, grant me the grace to desire it.

Acknowledgments

I would like to acknowledge the team at Catholic Mom.com, who encouraged me and helped to mold me in my faith. I would also like to thank my Cursillo prayer group for keeping me in prayerful company during the pandemic. You are an awesome group of ladies, and I love each one of you!

To the inspiring team at Marian Press, thank you for your graceful assistance in shepherding this book to publication.

To Dave Andrusko of *National Right to Life News:* thank you for your tutelage in matters of grammar and mission.

To Michael Ciccocioppo, thank you for your mentorship, which has made me a better writer and a more knowledgeable Catholic.

To my co-workers: many thanks for your faithful support during times of trial and tribulation. I am a better person for knowing and working with you.

To my daughter, Gabriella: I offer you my endless gratitude for your grace and your abundant love, which makes me want to dance with the angels.

And finally, to the Blessed Mother: thank you for watching over me, in all seasons, and for helping me to get to know your Son in a way I had not thought possible!

About the Author

 **Maria V. Gallagher** is an accomplished journalist whose work has received awards from the Associated Press, the Cleveland Press Club, the Society of Professional Journalists, and United Press International. Her radio work has been heard on AP Radio, NPR, Holy Family Radio, and JMJ Radio. An advocate for pregnant women and their children, Maria writes regularly for *National Right to Life News Today*. Maria is also active in the lay apostolate known as the worldwide Cursillo movement. The mother of a beautiful ballerina, Maria makes her home in central Pennsylvania.

Notes

[1] "The Song of Bernadette," www.imdb.com/title/tt0036377.

[2] "To Jesus Through Mary," diopitt.org/to-jesus-through-Mary.

[3] Luke 1:38, USCCB, bible.usccb.org/bible/luke/1.

[4] "Address of Pope Paul VI to Women," www.vatican.va/content/paul-vi/en/speeches/1965/documents/hf_p-vi_spe_19651208_epilogo-concilio-donne.html.

[5] Luke 1:26-27, USCCB, bible.usccb.org/bible/luke/1.

[6] *Catechism of the Catholic Church*, www.scborromeo.org/ccc/para/328.htm.

[7] Luke 1:28, USCCB, bible.usccb.org/bible/luke/1.

[8] Luke 1:29, *Ibid.*

[9] Luke 1:30, *Ibid.*

[10] Luke 1:31-33, *Ibid.*

[11] Luke 1:34, *Ibid.*

[12] Luke 1:35, *Ibid.*

[13] Luke 1:36-37, *Ibid.*

[14] Luke 1:38, *Ibid.*

[15] *Catechism of the Catholic Church*, www.scborromeo.org/ccc/para/1866.htm.

[16] Catholic Answers, www.catholic.com/encyclopedia/pride.

[17] Good Reads, www.goodreads.com/quotes/30608-i-m-a-little-pencil-in-the-hand-of-a-writing.

[18] "St. Catherine of Siena," dominicans.ie/st-catherine-of-siena.

[19] Catholic Online, www.catholic.org/saints/saint.php?saint_id=147.

[20] *Ibid.*

[21] *Ibid.*

[22] "Quotes by Bernadette Soubirous," www.biographyonline.net/spiritual/quotes/bernadette-soubirous-quotes.html.

[23] "5 Inspiring Quotes from St. Bernadette on Suffering and Humility," *Aleteia,* aleteia.org/2018/04/16/5-inspiring-quotes-from-st-bernadette-on-suffering-and-humility.

[24] *Ibid.*

[25] Catholic Link, catholic-link.org/quotes/st-bernadette-quote-shares-how-to-spend-your-time.

[26] Saintworks.net, saintsworks.net/forums/index.php?topic=2201.0;wap2.

[27] "New Michigan Laws Deter and Punish Coerced Abortion," Charlotte Lozier Institute, lozierinstitute.org/new-michigan-laws-deter-punish-coerced-abortion.

[28] Project Rachel, hopeafterabortion.com.

[29] National Cursillo Movement USA, www.natl-cursillo.org.

[30] Luke 1:39, USCCB, bible.usccb.org/bible/luke/1.

[31] Luke 1:40, *Ibid.*

[32] Luke 1:41, *Ibid.*

[33] Luke 1:41-42, *Ibid.*

[34] Luke 1:43, *Ibid.*

[35] Luke 1:46-48, *Ibid.*

[36] Luke 1:49-50, *Ibid.*

[37] Luke 1:51-52, *Ibid.*

[38] Luke 1:53-55, *Ibid.*

[39] "Pope Francis pleads with Catholics not to gossip," Catholic News Agency, catholicvoiceomaha.com/pope-francis-pleads-with-catholics-not-to-gossip/September 6, 2020.

[40] Mark 12:31, bible.usccb.org/bible/mark/12.

[41] Sister M. Callisita, MC, Mother Teresa Center, www.motherteresa.org.

[42] Catholic Online, www.catholic.org/saints/saint.php?saint_id=7252.

[43] *Ibid.*

[44] "7 Powerful Messages from Our Lady of Fatima: 'The Grace of God Will Be Your Comfort,'" www.churchpop.com/2019/05/13/7-powerful-messages-our-lady-of-fatima-gave-to-the-three-shepherd-children-pray-much-sacrifice-for-sinners.

[45] EWTN, www.ewtn.com/fatima/jacinta-marto.asp.

[46] "Saint of the Day," www.franciscanmedia.org/saint-of-the-day/saints-jacinta-and-francisco-marto.

[47] "Nebulizer," WebMd, www.webmd.com/asthma/guide/home-nebulizer-therapy.

[48] Luke 2:1-5, USCCB, bible.usccb.org/bible/luke/2.

[49] Luke 2: 6-7, *Ibid.*

[50] Luke 2:8-9, *Ibid.*

[51] Luke 2:10-14, *Ibid.*

[52] Luke 2:15-19, *Ibid.*

[53] Good Reads, www.goodreads.com/quotes/66880-christ-has-no-body-now-but-yours-no-hands-no.

[54] Catholic Online, www.catholic.org/saints/saint.php?saint_id=73.

55 *Ibid.*

56 "St. Juan Diego and Our Lady," www.catholiceducation.org/ en/culture/catholic-contributions/saint-juan-diego-and-our-lady.html.

57 *Ibid.*

58 See: BeginningCatholic.com, www.beginningcatholic.com/ sacraments.

59 Luke 2:22-24, USCCB, bible.usccb.org/bible/luke/2.

60 Luke 2:25-26, *Ibid.*

61 Luke 2:27-29, *Ibid.*

62 Luke 2:30-32, *Ibid.*

63 Luke 2:34-35, *Ibid.*

64 Luke 2:36-38, *Ibid.*

65 See: National Right to Life, www.nrlc.org/abortion/ diaryofanunbornchild.

66 National Right to Life, www.nationalrighttolifenews.org/ 2022/01/factsheet-reported-annual-abortions-1973-2019.

67 Catholic Online, www.catholic.org/saints/saint.php?saint_ id=105.

68 "36 Inspiring Quotes from St. Thérèse of Lisieux," dowym. com/voices/inspiring-quotes-from-st-therese-of-lisieux.

69 Catholic Online, www.catholic.org/saints/saint.php?saint_ id=105.

70 "36 Inspiring Quotes from St. Thérèse of Lisieux," dowym. com/voices/inspiring-quotes-from-st-therese-of-lisieux.

71 Catholic Online, www.catholic.org/saints/saint.php?saint_ id=105.

72 *Story of a Soul,* Thérèse of Lisieux, Our Sunday Visitor, 2018.

73 Good Reads, www.goodreads.com/author/quotes/248952. Th_r_se_de_Lisieux?page=1.

74 Author's private journal.

75 Luke 2:41-42, USCCB, bible.usccb.org/bible/luke/2.

76 Luke 2:43-45, *Ibid.*

77 Luke 2:46-47, *Ibid.*

78 Luke 2:48, *Ibid.*

79 Luke 2:49, *Ibid.*

80 Luke 2:51, *Ibid.*

81 Luke 2:52, *Ibid.*

82 Catholic Hymn, catholichymn.blogspot.com/2015/11/Jesus -My-Lord-My-God-My-All.html.

[83] "10 Quotes on Eucharistic Adoration from the Saints," www.catholic.sg/10-quotes-on-eucharistic-adoration-from-the-saints.

[84] *Ibid.*

[85] *Ibid.*

[86] *Ibid.*

[87] Catholic Online, www.catholic.org/saints/saint.php?saint_id=6985.

[88] *Ibid.*

[89] See: "Saint Gianna Beretta Molla," saintgianna.org/reflectionosst.htm.

[90] *Ibid.*

[91] "5 Inspirational Saint Gianna Molla Quotes," relevantradio.com/2018/04/5-inspirational-saint-gianna-molla-quotes.

[92] Catholic Online, www.catholic.org/saints/saint.php?saint_id=6985.

[93] See: "5 Inspirational Saint Gianna Molla Quotes," relevantradio.com/2018/04/5-inspirational-saint-gianna-molla-quotes.

[94] Busted Halo, bustedhalo.com/dailyjolt/we-always-find-that-those-who-walked-closest-to-christ-were-those-who-had-to-bear-the-greatest-trials-st-teresa-of-avila.